Effective Writing
in the Public Sector

D1564690

Effective Writing in the Public Sector

John W. Swain and Kathleen Dolan Swain

M.E.Sharpe
Armonk, New York
London, England

Library of Congress Cataloging-in-Publication Data

Swain, John W.
Effective writing in the public sector / by John W. Swain and Kathleen Dolan Swain.
  pages cm
  Includes bibliographical references and index.
  ISBN 978-0-7656-4149-6 (hardcover : alk. paper)—
  ISBN 978-0-7656-4150-2 (pbk. : alk. paper)
  1. Government report writing—Handbooks, manuals, etc. 2. Authorship—
Handbooks, manuals, etc. 3. Communication in public administration—Handbooks,
manuals, etc. I. Swain, Kathleen Dolan II. Title.

JF1525.R46S83 2014
808.06′6351—dc23   2013049798

Printed in the United States of America

GP (c)   10   9   8   7   6   5   4   3   2   1
GP (p)   10   9   8   7   6   5   4   3   2   1

We dedicate this book to James M. Banovetz, a singularly exceptional teacher. His integrity—both personal and professional—has affected us in ways even more profound than we realized when we were his students. Words cannot express the fullness of our debt to him.

Contents

Acknowledgments

We wish to thank all of the people who have aided us in producing this book. Our appreciation for their many contributions to this project is boundless.

We would like to acknowledge our teachers, students, colleagues, and the many practitioners from whom we have learned much about writing for the public sector. More specifically, we thank the following people for reading our original manuscript and for providing invaluable comments and insights that made the book better: Sheryl Gallaher, David Limardi, Dan Nisavic, Jim Norris, John Perry, Paul Peterson, and Dwight Vick.

We also thank Harry Briggs, executive editor extraordinaire at M. E. Sharpe, who believed in this project from the beginning and provided much-needed support and encouragement during the process. We are also indebted to Elizabeth Parker, associate editor, for her valuable assistance and to Laura Brengelman, assistant managing editor and project editor, for her superb efforts to make this book the best it could be. We truly appreciate, too, the fine work of copyeditor Deborah Ring.

Last, but certainly not least, we thank our family members and the many others who have encouraged us while we worked on this book.

Introduction

We designed this book for students and practitioners in public administration because of the unique challenges they face in their everyday writing. In many ways, of course, students and practitioners in public administration experience the same concerns as all writers. To write effectively, all writers need to understand whom they are writing to so they can express themselves clearly to that particular audience; be familiar with and use the proper form of writing for the situation; observe the rules of English grammar, punctuation, and spelling; and follow conventions on language usage.

But the writing done by individuals working in the public sector also differs in critical ways. One difference is the need to communicate with a wide range of audiences. Public sector audiences range from an individual citizen, to special-interest groups, to technical specialists, to the public at large. As such, people who write for the public sector face the challenge of communicating the right information in the right tone to the right audience. For example, a letter to a citizen about a zoning change will differ greatly in content, language, and tone from a letter to the members of a zoning commission, even though the general topic is the same.

The types of communications written by individuals in the public sector also span a broader range than those of other writers—even more so than the public relations departments of private businesses. Because public sector officials write for all of the public, they must spread their communications across a wide range of media in a wide range of forms. A village manager, for example, may have to write not only memos and letters but also public service announcements and formal reports. That manager and staff might also be involved in writing rules and grant applications.

Another special concern of public sector writers is the importance of their communications to the public. Public communications may literally involve life-and-death situations. For example, a communication written about an immediate health hazard to the community must be clear and concise to effect the right results. Other communications affect other aspects of a community's well-being. Public officials and staff are responsible for writing about such varied concerns as crime prevention and tax assessments, for example, and all such writing places a premium on clarity.

Public sector writers face two additional challenges. First, many people distrust government communications. In some cases people react adversely to government communications that affect them in a negative way, for example, an order to cease business. In such communications, governments express their power to coerce, and the writing must be approached and expressed with this in mind.

Second, much government writing historically has been characterized, justly so, as "bureaucratese"—a foggy, pretentious, and jargon-infested way of writing that baffles (and annoys, as we can testify) the people trying to read the communication. Here is a good example of bureaucratese: "Upon receipt of this memo dated 28 June 2013, affected parties are notified that the new book deposit process will be effectuated immediately. Affected persons with questions, concerns, or comments should contact our office at their earliest possible convenience." How much better it would have been to state, "The new book deposit process starts now. Please contact our office if you have questions or comments." Bureaucratese has persisted throughout all levels of government because of habit and lack of knowledge of how to write in a better way. We hope this book will help writers avoid the convoluted writing that frustrates so many readers.

Writing effectively contributes to the success of individuals, governments, and the public at large. Students who write effectively earn better grades. Practitioners who write effectively are likely to gain positive attention and promotions. Governments with officials and staff who write effectively more ably serve their publics—and that means all of us benefit, a worthy endeavor indeed.

We developed this book so it can be used as both a learning tool and a resource guide. Each chapter in Part I covers an aspect of basic writing that public sector writers need to understand to communicate effectively. In this part, therefore, we present in detail the topics discussed above: determining your audience and adapting your writing to that audience; understanding the most common forms of communication found in the public sector and how to use them; reviewing the basic rules of English grammar and how to apply them; learning how to write more clearly and concisely; and proofreading your writing to be sure you have expressed yourself clearly and correctly.

Part II provides a more detailed look at the specific forms of writing used to communicate with public audiences. In addition to discussing such basic forms as memos and letters, in this section we delve into such types of communication as e-mails, media releases, public service announcements, and newsletters.

Part III focuses on specific forms of writing used to communicate with internal and technical audiences. For example, we discuss formal reports, types of proposals, budget justifications, and rules.

The appendixes are designed as resource guides. For example, in Appendix A you will find lists of commonly misspelled words along with the correct spellings, commonly misused words and their proper usage, and replacements for gender-specific words. Appendix B provides samples of two major documentation styles commonly used in formal writing. Appendix C provides answers to the exercises we include at the end of each chapter.

The book is rounded off with an annotated bibliography of other useful resources, including published articles and books as well as selected websites. We also provide a comprehensive index to help guide your way.

We hope all these materials will help you develop your skills as a writer.

Part I

The Basic Components

1

Essential Preliminary Steps to Effective Writing

As you probably gathered from our discussion in the introduction, the act of writing begins even before we pick up a pen or pencil or place our hands on the keyboard. To craft an effective message, a writer must take four preliminary steps:

- *Why:* Determine the purpose of your message.
- *Who:* Identify your audience and the proper tone for that audience.
- *Which:* Decide which form of writing is best in this situation.
- *How:* Consider how to prepare your message in the most effective way.

Each of these steps is described in turn below.

Step 1: Determine the Purpose of Your Message

Purposes can be put into two broad categories: writing to *inform* and writing to *persuade*. There is an easy way to determine your purpose. You simply ask yourself, "Why am I writing this message?" For example, are you writing to tell an individual or a group what transpired at a staff meeting? Are you writing to your immediate supervisor about an idea you have to streamline an office procedure?

The first message is intended to inform; the second is an effort to persuade someone else to consider your point of view. The construction of your message will vary depending on what your purpose is:

- If your goal is to *inform*: Put the most important information at the beginning of the message.
- If your goal is to *persuade*: First present the problem and then propose your solution. Explain why you think the problem is a problem, why your solution will solve the problem, and how you would proceed to carry out the solution to the problem.

Example: Message to Inform

Dear Karen:

I will not be able to attend the meeting today because of a prior commitment. I will be in touch with you tomorrow to find out what was discussed.

Sincerely,

Lou

Example: Message to Persuade

Dear Janet:

In reviewing the latest figures from the accounting department, I noticed that we again are very close to going over our monthly budget for office supplies. As in the past four months, most of the expenditures went toward the repair and maintenance of our photocopier.

In conducting research into how to solve this problem, I located a photocopier at HMS Office Supply Store that is being offered at a discount because this particular model is being phased out.

The purchase price is $1,200. Even though the initial outlay for purchasing this new photocopier would cause us to go over budget, I think that in the long run this acquisition would be cost-effective. We would save not only in terms of eliminating the costly repairs the old machine requires (an average of $125 a month for the past four months alone) but also in terms of staff time now spent dealing with problems with the old machine.

Could we meet tomorrow to discuss this option?

Sincerely,

Carlos

Step 2: Identify Your Audience and the Proper Tone

Once you have determined the purpose of your writing, you need to think about whom you are writing to and craft your message to that audience. If you do not address the right people, your message will lose much of its impact. In a very helpful chart in *Plain Language in Government Writing*, Judith Gillespie Myers groups public sector audiences into four main types: managers, experts or advisors, operators, and general readers.[1] We agree in general with her groups but would categorize the four types as follows:

- Decision makers
- Staff members
- Experts
- General public

Examples of *decision makers* are elected executives, appointed chief executives, and department managers. Overall, decision makers supervise others and decide how public organizations will act.

Staff members include people on the front lines of an organization and those who provide services to support them. Frontline staff members include teachers, postal workers, and firefighters; examples of support staff members are personnel clerks, finance clerks, and administrative assistants.

Experts can be internal or external to the organization. Examples include civil engineers, scientists, attorneys, and planners.

The *general public* can be defined as those people outside a public organization who have a need for the services provided by the organization or who have an interest in the organization's goals and values. The scope of the public being addressed can range from very broad (for example, all citizens of a city) to moderate (for example, residents in a park and recreation district) to narrow (residents of a neighborhood or even a single individual).

Once you have identified your audience, you can set the tone of your message on the basis of your audience's general characteristics. The table below lists each group's general characteristics and the appropriate tone for each audience.

Type of Audience	General Characteristics	Tone
Decision makers	Broad perspective; relate the organization to a larger environment; most interested in information necessary to make decisions	Short, to the point, formal language
Staff members	Narrower perspective related to specific work responsibilities and personal situation; can only be expected to know their own jobs; looking for information related to their job and personal situation	Light, not as formal
Experts	Very narrow perspective; concerned about their area of expertise; looking for information specifically related to their area of expertise	Formal but more detailed than for decision makers
General public	Varied perspectives; lack in-depth knowledge of subjects and terms; looking for information that affects their personal lives	Conversational and explanatory

In the following examples, we can see how one topic—an organization moving to a new office—is approached differently depending on the audience that is being addressed.

Example: Memo to a Decision Maker

To: Peter
From: Robin
Date: August 6, 2014
Subject: Relocation Date

All preliminary work on the relocation of the staff to the new offices has been completed, and we have set a date of August 14 for the final move. You can now notify staff members.

If you have any questions, please let me know.

As you can see, this memo is short and provides only a broad overview of the subject.

Example: Memo to Staff

To: All Department Heads
From: Peter Piperman, Village Manager
Date: August 6, 2014
Subject: Relocation Date

It's official—our new building is ready! We will start our move on August 14. Please plan to meet in the conference room at 9:00 a.m. on August 13 to review our plans.

Thanks for your continuing efforts as we make this move.

Even though this memo is also short, you can see a major difference in tone from the preceding example. This less formal tone fits well with the concept of a team approach to managing staff.

Example: Memo to Expert

To: Joe Lombardi, Crew Chief
From: Robin Mann, Project Manager
Date: August 7, 2014
Subject: Certification Request Form for the New Building

As soon as you can, please send me a copy of the certification request form from the ADA that shows the requirements to be in compliance with the specs in Title III. I will then make the certification request and supporting materials available for public inspection.

Thank you.

Here we see a memo with much more technical information, including some terminology that the expert will already be familiar with.

Example: Letter to General Public

Village of Smithtown
578 Lee Road
Smithtown, Illinois 60006

August 6, 2014

Mr. and Mrs. Jack Waters
424 Eastern Way
Smithtown, Illinois 60006

Dear Mr. and Mrs. Waters:

We are pleased to announce that the building that will house the new administrative offices for the Village of Smithtown has been completed. Our new address will be 364 Village Lane.

Telephone numbers will not change. We will start moving on August 14 and plan to be open for business beginning at 9:00 a.m. on August 18.

We will keep our office on Lee Road open during the transition, so if you need to contact any village official during the time of the move, please feel free to get in touch with us there.

Thank you again for your tremendous support during this time of change. We look forward to serving you in our new offices!

Sincerely,

Judith Griffin
Mayor

This letter to the public (the reason for writing a letter instead of a memo is discussed in Chapter 5) contains all the information that citizens will need to continue communications with their local officials. The tone is more formal than the memo to the staff but is not overly stuffy and avoids jargon.

Note: Always remember that no matter which audience you address and which tone you adopt, any written communication can find its way into the public arena. Indeed, every communication written by a public official or staff member is ultimately a public document under the various freedom of information acts (sometimes referred to as open records acts or sunshine acts), and thus the audience may be the media and every member of the community at large. It is therefore vitally important to take care in what and how you write and how you present your organization.

Step 3: Decide Which Form Is Best

We discuss forms of writing in more detail later in this book. Here we simply note that a great deal of public sector writing involves four basic forms: memos, letters, electronic messages, and reports.

Each of these forms has its own characteristics and purposes, as shown below.

Memos	Brief messages, usually between people in the same organization
Letters	Longer, more in-depth, and more formal correspondence, usually from someone in the organization to individual(s) outside the organization
Electronic messages	Usually communicated in e-mail format; somewhat less formal than memos; used to communicate both with people in the same organization and with persons outside
Reports	Presentation of facts given in a logical sequence; written for the public or for internal audiences and/or technical specialists

You saw examples of memos and a letter earlier in this chapter (see examples under Step 2). You might notice now that they indeed have distinct characteristics. The memos have "To," "From," "Date," and "Subject" lines; they are brief; and they are sent to colleagues in the organization. The letter, on the other hand, is much more formal. It is presented on letterhead and addressed to someone outside the organization. The tone, as might be expected, is also more formal than the tone in the memos.

No matter what the form of your message is, however, a communication is effective only if it is first well prepared. Let us turn to that step.

Step 4: Consider How to Prepare Your Message

Finally, before you begin the actual writing process, you need to think about how to prepare your message so you can present the most effective communication possible. This preparation involves answering two questions:

- What content should I include in my message?
- How should this content be presented?

The best way to prepare your message so that it has all the content you need to include and presents that content in an effective manner is to follow these two steps: (1) brainstorm (write down ideas as they come to you) and (2) organize.

Brainstorm

You can guide yourself through the brainstorming process in various ways, but the one we recommend for public sector writers is to adopt what journalists call the "5 Ws and 1 H." That is, to get started, write down the answers to the following questions:

- *Who* is involved in this situation?
- *What* is going to happen/has happened?
- *Where* is it going to happen/did it happen?
- *When* is it happening/did it happen?
- *Why* is it happening/did it happen?
- *How* is it happening/did it happen?

We would also add the following question—a critical one when working in the public sector:

- *What does this mean to the person reading the communication?*

Now let us take a topic and brainstorm. Say you need to write a letter to the general public regarding a new leaf collection program the village is adopting. (Note that at this point, we have completed Steps 1–3: we know the purpose of the correspondence [to inform], the audience [the general public], and the form [a letter].) We brainstorm by writing down the following:

- *Who:* The village, all the citizens of the village
- *What:* A new leaf collection program
- *Where:* Throughout the village
- *When:* November 3, 2014
- *Why:* Improve efficiency
- *How:* New bags, new collection dates
- *What does this mean to me:* Citizens need to take new actions to get leaves picked up

We need to emphasize one other point here—even though the purpose of your letter is to inform the village citizens of something, you also need to take into consideration an important facet of human nature: some people do not like change, and even more people do not like change when it causes them to do something different from what they are used to doing. This point is highlighted in the brainstorming process when we answer the "What does this mean to me" question and see the words "new" and "actions." Thus, even though our purpose is to inform (and therefore the most important information is placed at the beginning of the message), we also need to focus attention on the "why," that is, why this new program is better for everyone (it improves efficiency). Your letter, then, will contain the answers to all the questions listed above but also will include additional information about "why" and "what does this mean to me."

Now that you have brainstormed and know what information needs to go into your letter, you can move to the next step in the preparation process: organizing your thoughts into an effective message.

Organize

One of the best ways to organize your thoughts is to get out a new piece of paper, pick up that pen or pencil again, and write out your main ideas in outline form. Each outline should have the following components:

- Introduction
- Body
- Conclusion

The main purpose of an outline is to help you get your thoughts in proper order so that the reader of your message can easily follow what you are trying to say. The outline is a tremendous help because it causes you to think in terms of order.

In the introduction, you explain why you are writing your message. In the body, you present the point or points you are writing about. In the conclusion, you sum up the main points and suggest further action (if applicable).

Using the ideas we created in the brainstorming session, we can now structure them:

Example: Outline of a Letter to Residents to Explain the New Leaf Collection Program

1. Explain why letter is being written [*Introduction*]
2. Describe former system [*Body*]
   A. Specific method adopted
   B. Why it no longer works well
3. Describe new system
   A. Specific method adopted
   B. Why it is an improvement on old system
4. Express appreciation for cooperation [*Conclusion*]

The example below shows the letter we wrote as a result of the brainstorming and organizing process.

Example: Letter to Residents to Explain the New Leaf Collection Program

Village of Hanville
348 South Pine Street
Hanville, Illinois 60004

Office of the Mayor

October 6, 2014

Dear Resident:

Greetings. I am pleased to announce that our new leaf collection program is set to begin on Monday, November 3, 2014.

As you all know, our former system of raking leaves into the street had begun to create problems. When that program was implemented in 1980, we had only 250 citizens, and the system worked efficiently. With the village population now reaching 1,100, however, resulting in an increase in new homes, new trees, and thus new leaves, we have seen that having so many leaves raked into the street has caused flooding and traffic problems, leading to safety concerns.

After careful study by the Public Works Department, we have endorsed the new plan whereby all residents will place their leaves in specially designated bags (see attached picture). These bags are available for purchase at all local hardware stores and grocery supermarkets. The bags should be placed with your garbage and recyclables for collection on your regularly scheduled garbage collection day. This new system will allow us to reduce the flooding and traffic hazards we have been experiencing because of the old program.

Thank you to everyone involved in this effort to keep our village rated the cleanest village in the south suburban area!

Sincerely,

Mayor Arbor

Now that you have taken the preliminary steps, you are ready for the next major challenge—the actual writing. Your correspondence will already be improved because you know your purpose, your audience, your form, and the organization of your content. Three other elements are also crucial, though.

First, you must get the mechanics right; that is, you must be sure that the correspondence contains correct spelling, punctuation, and sentence construction. As a reader, you know that when you read something that has misspellings, incorrect punctuation, or poor construction, you start to question the credibility of the entire message—and the messenger. Second, you need to polish your writing. Third, you need to proofread it. We discuss these three elements in the remainder of this section.

Key Points of Chapter 1

Before you begin writing, you need to identify the
following:

- The purpose of your message
- Your audience and what tone your message should take
- Which form you should use
- What content you should include in your message

EXERCISES FOR CHAPTER 1

Exercise 1.1

Read the following passage and then answer the questions that
follow it.

Get involved in making the environment healthy! Plant a tree in
your yard or help others plant trees. Trees help in the following
ways:

- Trees in your yard can increase your home's value by up to
15 percent.
- Trees conserve energy in the winter by slowing down those
cold winds.
- Trees conserve energy in the summer by shading your home
from the sun, thus reducing your air-conditioning bills.
- Trees help the air—they produce the oxygen we breathe,
and they filter the particulates in the air.

Call now to get started. Our telephone number is (652) 555-
0961.

Questions

    a. What is the general purpose of this message?
    b. Who is the audience?
    c. Is the message effective? Why or why not?

Exercise 1.2

Read the following passage and then answer the questions that follow it.

> The Municipality anticipates that the contract for the preparation of the EA will be approved and implemented by July 2015. For Barn Road Project #02-433, pending state DOT approval, the Municipality and the Skyler Engineering Firm, LLC, will execute the necessary steps to contract (10 percent local match) for an Environmental Assessment (EA) in accordance with the work scope approved by the state DOT on June 5, 2014. It is estimated that the EA will be completed in 18 months.

Questions

    a. What is the general purpose of this message?
    b. Who is the audience?
    c. Is the message organized well? Why or why not?

Answers can be found in Appendix C.

2

The Mechanics of Writing

A Refresher Course on the Basic Rules of English

Because the basic rules of English can be rather complicated and because one of the major goals of this book is to make writing less complicated, in this chapter we provide an overview of the most important fundamentals of English. You can obtain more extensive information in the many excellent resource materials that are available in bookstores and libraries and on the Internet; several of these resources are listed in the annotated bibliography at the end of this book. Here we review the most important aspects for public sector writers: spelling, punctuation, and sentence construction.

Spelling

Perhaps the most important rule to remember with regard to spelling is the following: when in doubt, *check a dictionary*. Note, too, that the word "dictionary" here means either a formal dictionary you hold in your hands or a reputable online dictionary. In other words, *do not rely* solely on computer spell-checker programs. These programs are extremely limited; they can indicate misspellings, but they cannot tell whether a word is used incorrectly.

For example, the English language is full of words called *homonyms*, that is, words that sound the same—and sometimes are even spelled the same way—but have different meanings. For example, we have, just to name a few, aid/aide, bite/byte, forth/fourth, and their/they're/there. Table A.1 in Appendix A lists some of the most common homonyms we encounter on a daily basis. As you can see, *their are many words that can altar you're meaning when not spelled rite, aren't they're?*

Other words are simply difficult to spell. Table A.2 in Appendix A lists words that are frequently misspelled.

Hint: In addition to using a dictionary, you might want to use the following method: break the difficult word into syllables and then say each of the syllables out loud. Both seeing and hearing the word separated by syllables can help you determine its accuracy—and find it more easily in the dictionary.

Punctuation

One best-selling nonfiction book published a few years ago was titled *Eats, Shoots and Leaves: The Zero Tolerance Approach to Punctuation* by Lynne Truss. The title comes from the following story:

> A panda walks into a café. He orders a sandwich, eats it, then draws a gun and fires two shots in the air.
>
> "Why?" asks the confused waiter, as the panda makes towards the exit. The panda produces a badly punctuated wildlife manual and tosses it over his shoulder.
>
> "I'm a panda," he says at the door. "Look it up."
>
> The waiter turns to the relevant entry and, sure enough, finds an explanation.
>
> "*Panda.* Large black-and-white bear-like mammal, native to China. Eats, shoots and leaves."[1]

This account is a wonderfully clever way to illustrate the importance of punctuation marks and their proper placement in sentences. Moreover, the fact that the book was a best seller shows that many people are confused about how to use punctuation marks correctly. Punctuation marks serve a vital purpose in writing: they indicate stops and pauses, what information belongs together, and the mood of the writer. There are numerous punctuation marks in the English language, but here we focus on the main ones used by public sector writers. These punctuation marks are the period, comma, semicolon, colon, question mark, exclamation point, parentheses, brackets, quotation marks, and apostrophe.

The Period (.)

The period is the most common punctuation mark. It is used to indicate the end of a full sentence—that is, a sentence with a subject and a verb that expresses a complete thought.

> The board met in a closed session to discuss personnel issues.

Note, too, that a period is occasionally used after single words or phrases, primarily when the writer or speaker is being emphatic.

> Will I give in? Absolutely not.

There is an exception to the rule regarding the period: when you give a list, you do not need to add a period after the items in the list unless the items are complete sentences.

> We brought the following to the meeting:
> an agenda
> a proposal from the Library Board
> an Environmental Impact Statement

Compare this to the following example, in which all items are complete sentences.

> To print a document in this program, use the following steps:
>
> 1. Click on "File" in the main menu.
> 2. Click on "Print."
> 3. Choose the range of pages you wish to print.
> 4. Choose the number of copies you wish to print.
> 5. Click on "Print."

The Comma (,)

Commas are used to indicate pauses of different types. The rules regarding commas are numerous; we list the main ones below.

Rule 1

Use a comma to separate independent clauses linked by "and," "but," "or," "nor," "yet," and "so" (coordinating conjunctions). The term "independent clauses" means that each clause has a subject and verb and could stand alone as a sentence in its own right.

> The trustees voted to pass the ordinance, and they discussed pending zoning matters.

> Residents are allowed to build fences, but they must first receive approval from the village.

In each of these examples, the clauses could also stand alone as complete sentences ("The trustees voted to pass the ordinance." "They discussed pending zoning matters."). When the sentences are joined by "and" or "but," a comma must be added before the coordinating conjunction.

Note: Do not use a comma to join an independent clause to a dependent clause.

> The trustees voted and then adjourned.

Here, the first part of the sentence can stand alone ("The trustees voted"), but the second part ("then adjourned) is not a complete sentence because it has no subject.

Note: Do not use a comma to join two independent clauses without a coordinating conjunction.

> The voters went to the polls, the majority voted for the incumbent.

Without a coordinating conjunction (in this case, the word "and") in this sentence, we have what is called a "run-on sentence." (We discuss run-on sentences in more detail later in this chapter.)

Rule 2

As the excerpt from *Eats, Shoots and Leaves* shows, the placement of commas is critical to meaning. Use a comma to separate each item in a series of three or more items, including a comma (sometimes referred to as the "serial comma") before the conjunction.

> They could not decide whether to order fish, chicken, or pasta
> for the banquet.

In some professions, primarily journalism, the last comma is not added. The argument is that this comma is not necessary most of the time. Sometimes, however, the omission can make the meaning of a sentence unclear.

> We talked to the village manager, a restaurant owner and a
> former teacher.

In this example, we do not know whether the writer is referring to one person (a village manager who is also a restaurant owner and former teacher) or three people (a village manager, a restaurant owner, and a former teacher).

If the writer is referring to just one person, the sentence should be reworded to clarify. One possibility is as follows:

> We talked to the village manager, who is also a restaurant
> owner and a former teacher.

If the writer is referring to three people, a comma should be added before the "and" to clarify:

> We talked to the village manager, a restaurant owner, and a
> former teacher.

Hint: Try to read what you have written as someone else might read it. Such a practice can help clarify ambiguities.

Rule 3

Use a comma after a long introductory phrase.

> At Monday evening's board meeting, the finance director accepted the employee-of-the-year award.

Note: Also use a comma after a short introductory phrase if the sentence would be confusing without it.

> To John, Martin had been the ideal employee.

Rule 4

Use a comma to set off nonessential elements in a sentence. This rule gets into the sometimes subtle distinction between restrictive and nonrestrictive clauses, which is difficult for many writers to understand. A word or phrase is *restrictive* if the sentence cannot be understood properly without it, that is, if it identifies the thing being described or discussed. A word or phrase is *nonrestrictive* (not essential) if the sentence can be understood correctly without the additional word or phrase.

> Bill's son Henry decided to run for a seat on the city council.

In this example, the word "Henry" is restrictive—that is, essential to the meaning of the sentence—because in this case Bill has several other sons, but only Henry is running for a seat on the city council. No comma is placed either before or after the name because the word is needed to understand which son is being discussed.

Compare this example to the following:

> Mike's wife, Linda, became manager of the credit union.

Here, the word "Linda" is not essential to the meaning of the sentence because Mike has (we hope) only one wife. Her name is simply additional information and is therefore set off by commas.

The distinction between restrictive and nonrestrictive can become more troublesome when using phrases starting with "that" and "which."

> The department developed a plan that will reduce the cost of recycling.

In this sentence, no comma is added before the word "that" because the clause ("that will reduce the cost of recycling") is needed to identify the plan being described.

Contrast this example with the following:

> The Village of South Chicago Heights, which is located in the south suburban area of Chicago, has a population of about four thousand people.

Here the phrase "which is located in the south suburban area of Chicago" is set off by commas because it is not essential; it simply adds information.

Hint: Generally speaking, "that" is used to restrict, and "which" is used nonrestrictively. Therefore, if you are going to set off a clause with commas, start with "which." Otherwise, use "that."

The Semicolon (;)

The semicolon indicates a harder pause than the comma, and it is used to link two independent clauses not already joined by a coordinating conjunction. Semicolons tend to be used between independent clauses that are closely linked, as in a sentence that expresses a cause-and-effect relationship.

> The bus is late; we will not get to the office on time.

Note that a period could also be used after "late" ("The bus is late. We will not get to the office on time."). The semicolon, however, links the two thoughts more closely.

The Colon (:)

The colon signals that what follows is closely related to or explains what has just been said. Between two independent clauses, it signals a more forceful pause than a semicolon.

> You must act immediately: lives are at stake.

The colon is also used to introduce a list.

> Budget hearings will be held on the following days: September 26, October 6, and October 15.

Note: Generally speaking, do not place a colon directly after a verb or a preposition.

> *Incorrect:* The study involved: marketing, public relations, and production.

> *Correct:* The study involved three departments: marketing, public relations, and production.

The Question Mark (?)

A question mark is used to indicate a direct question.

> What time is the meeting?

A question mark can also be used to indicate surprise or uncertainty.

> This is true?

Do not add a question mark when writing an indirect question.

Where he was going was the question at the meeting.

The Exclamation Point (!)

The exclamation point seems to have found new popularity in e-mail and text messages. It should be used sparingly, however, because it loses its effectiveness when inserted too often. An exclamation point is generally used for emphasis.

Maria thought we could not get it finished on time, but we did!

A direct question can be changed into an exclamatory sentence with the use of an exclamation point. The change is usually made to indicate emphasis.

How could you say that!

Parentheses and Brackets (( ), [ ])

Parentheses are usually used to set off additional explanatory or qualifying information.

Tanika sent the bill to the attorney's office (the case involved the dispute between the Tates and the City of Summerville).

We worked all night on the GIS (Geographic Information System).

Brackets are generally used to indicate parenthetical information within parentheses.

(Fire Station 2 [located at 231 First Street] is being renovated.)

Most confusion regarding parentheses has to do with the placement of ending punctuation marks (the period, question mark, and exclamation point) in a sentence with parentheses—that is, whether these marks should be placed inside or outside the closing parenthesis. The following rules apply.

Rule 1

When you place the parenthetical information in a separate sentence, start the sentence with a capital letter and place the ending punctuation *inside* the closing parenthesis.

> The president's term is four years. (Each board member's term is two years, though.)

Rule 2

When you place the parenthetical information within a sentence, start the parenthetical sentence or phrase with a lowercase letter and place the ending punctuation *outside* the ending parenthesis.

> Even though he was not feeling well, Dominick came to work (he stayed for just four hours, however).

Note: There is an exception to these rules when the information within the parentheses is a question or an exclamation. In these cases, the question mark or exclamation point goes inside the ending parenthesis, but an ending punctuation mark is still placed at the end of the sentence.

> The police responded quickly (do you think they expected trouble?).

> Peter worked the overtime requested (he was not happy about it, however!).

Quotation Marks (" ")

Quotation marks are used to indicate direct quotations or words used in a special way.

> Governor Bayer said, "I come here today to celebrate a new beginning."

> The city is divided into areas called "wards."

Quotation marks are also used to express irony or doubt.

> The "brief" meeting actually went on for more than an hour.

Note: Be careful not to overuse quotation marks in this way. As with exclamation points, overuse causes quotation marks to lose their effectiveness (in addition to becoming annoying to the reader).

As with parentheses and brackets, some confusion exists regarding the placement of ending punctuation marks with quotation marks. The following rules apply.

Rule 1

Periods are placed *inside* the ending quotation mark.

> Mick agreed with the adage that "a rolling stone gathers no moss."

Rule 2

When only the quoted material itself is a question or exclamation, the question mark or exclamation point goes *inside* the ending quotation mark.

> The budget director asked, "Where are those numbers?"

> It is true—Elena yelled, "Let me through; I can help!"

Rule 3

When the entire sentence is a question or an exclamation, the question mark or exclamation point goes *outside* the ending quotation mark.

> Where was the budget director when he said, "Give me those numbers"?

> I strongly agree—"Give me liberty or give me death"!

The Apostrophe (')

The apostrophe is another of those pesky punctuation marks that seems to cause a tremendous amount of difficulty. Apostrophes are used both to show possession and to indicate the omission of a letter or letters in a contraction. The general rules are as follows.

Rule 1

To show possession of a singular subject, add " 's."

> Ellen's efforts led to her promotion.

This rule applies even if the singular subject ends in an "s."

> Dennis's office is at the end of the hallway.

Rule 2

To show possession of a plural subject, place the apostrophe after the "s."

> Both departments' contracts expire at the end of this month.

Note that this rule is true even when adding the apostrophe to a plural subject that already has an "s" or "es" added to make it plural.

> The Stevenses' address is in the book.

Rule 3

Add an apostrophe when using the contraction of a word.

It's scheduled for 4:00 p.m. [It's = It is]

We're on our way to the meeting. [We're = We are]

Note: Some people get confused about the difference between contractions and possessive pronouns ("his," "hers," "its," "my," "our," "your," "their") and when to use each. It might help to remember that a contraction is a shortened form; some letter or letters are missing, and the apostrophe stands in for the letter or letters. When using a possessive pronoun, however, no apostrophe is needed. "Its" does not mean "It is."

Its cost is too high. [*Not* "It is cost is too high."]

Your help was invaluable. [*Not* "You are help was invaluable."]

Hint: Avoid contractions in formal writing, such as letters and reports.

Sentence Construction

At its most basic level, a sentence is constructed correctly when it expresses a complete thought and contains a subject, a verb that indicates an action by or toward the subject, and a punctuation mark to indicate where the complete thought ends. A properly constructed sentence can even contain just two words. For example, consider the sentence "Rebecca smiled." The sentence has a subject (Rebecca) performing an action (smiled) and contains an ending punctuation mark (the period). The sentence also makes sense when we read it.

Constructing a sentence correctly becomes a little more complicated when we add more words to the sentence, as inadvertent errors can then occur. In this section we describe some of the more common errors in sentence construction: sentence fragments; run-on sentences; subject-verb disagreement; subject-pronoun disagreement; lack of parallelism; and dangling modifiers. Note that all these problems are errors in sentence construction; we deal more with the art of sentence construction in the next chapter.

Sentence Fragments

As noted above, formal written English requires complete sentences, that is, sentences that contain both a subject and a verb *and* can stand alone.

> The cleaning crew finished on time.

Here, the subject is "crew," and the verb is "finished." The sentence is complete as written. Trouble with sentence fragments usually occurs when writers add words or create clauses that cannot stand alone.

> *Fragment:* Although the task was difficult.

In this example, even though there is a subject ("task") and a verb ("was"), because of the subordinating word "Although," the reader is left wondering what happened. In this case the writer needs to either eliminate the subordinating word or add the subordinate clause to an independent clause to make a full sentence.

> *Correct:* The task was difficult.

> *Correct:* Although the task was difficult, the cleaning crew finished on time.

The best way to tell whether you have a sentence fragment is to see whether the sentence starts with a subordinating word (such as "although," "because," "if," "since," "while," "who," "which," and "that"). In those situations, as noted in the above example, be sure to either delete the subordinating word or join the fragment to an independent clause to create a complete sentence.

Run-On Sentences

Two types of run-on sentences are common. In the first type, a sentence is not correct because it has two main clauses joined only by a comma.

> *Run-on sentence:* The budget director just signed off on the bid, it will go before the full board tomorrow.

This sentence needs either (1) a connecting word or (2) a stronger punctuation mark so the reader understands that two main ideas are being presented.

> *Corrected sentence:* The budget director just signed off on the bid, and it will go before the full board tomorrow.

> *Corrected sentence:* The budget director just signed off on the bid; it will go before the full board tomorrow.

> *Corrected sentence:* The budget director just signed off on the bid. It will go before the full board tomorrow.

In the second type of run-on sentence, the writer neglects to place any coordinating word or punctuation mark between the two independent clauses.

> *Run-on sentence:* The police department was short-staffed the chief agreed to hire a community service officer to assist the regular officers.

This sentence needs either (1) a comma and connecting word or (2) a semicolon or period to separate the clauses.

> *Corrected sentence:* The police department was short-staffed, so the chief agreed to hire a community service officer to assist the regular officers.

> *Corrected sentence:* The police department was short-staffed; the chief agreed to hire a community service officer to assist the regular officers.

Corrected sentence: The police department was short-staffed. The chief agreed to hire a community service officer to assist the regular officers.

Note that in the above example (and in all sentences of this type), you could make one of the clauses a dependent clause and tie it to the independent clause with a comma.

Correct sentence: Because the police department was short-staffed, the chief agreed to hire a community service officer to assist them.

Subject-Verb Disagreement

Particular types of sentences require that you double-check to be sure the subject and the verb in the sentence agree in number. In the first type, a group of words comes between the subject and its verb, making it more difficult to determine whether the subject is singular or plural (and thus uses a singular or plural verb, respectively). The easiest way to determine the subject in this type of sentence is to mentally ignore any modifiers.

Public hearings on the proposed zoning change were held on two consecutive Tuesdays.

In this sentence the subject is "hearings" (the phrase "on the proposed zoning change" is just describing [or modifying] which hearings), so the verb must also be plural ("were held," not "was held").

A second type of sentence to double-check is one in which the sentence is inverted—that is, the verb comes before the subject in the sentence.

Down the street are the civic center and the county jail.

At first glance, one might think that the subject of the sentence is "street" and that the verb should therefore be singular ("is").

This sentence is inverted, however. Once you read the sentence for meaning, you realize the writer is saying that the civic center and the county jail are down the street. This sentence has a plural subject ("the civic center and the county jail") and thus takes a plural verb ("are").

Another type of inverted sentence can also cause difficulty. When we start a sentence with such words as "It is," "There is," and "There are"—formally known as *expletives* (that is, meaningless words)—we are actually creating an inverted sentence because "It is," "There is," and "There are" are just filler words—they help fill in the sentence but do not by themselves add meaning to the sentence. For example, if we write, "There is money in the petty cash drawer," we mean that money is in the petty cash drawer. The intended subject is "money," not "There."

Be especially careful in this regard when you have a plural subject. For example, the sentence "There is both the mayor and the city council to consider" is incorrect because the intended subject of the sentence is plural, but the verb is singular. That is, what the writer means here is that both the mayor and the city council need to be considered; this plural subject therefore requires a plural verb. The correct sentence would read, "There are both the mayor and the city council to consider."

Note: We have more to say about starting sentences with "It is," "There is," and "There are" in the next chapter.

A third type of sentence in which subject-verb agreement should always be double-checked is one in which the subjects are joined by "or," "nor," or the "either . . . or"/"neither . . . nor" combination. In such sentences, the rule to remember is that the verb should agree with the part of the subject that is closest to the verb.

Incorrect: Neither Julio nor his assistants was at the meeting.

Correct: Neither Julio nor his assistants were at the meeting.

Because the subject closer to the verb is "assistants," the verb is plural.

Hint: If one subject is singular and the other is plural, try to place the plural subject last to avoid having the sentence look and sound awkward.

Subject-Pronoun Disagreement

When writing, always be sure that any pronoun you use ("he," "she," or "it," for example) to refer to the noun agrees in number with the noun.

> *Incorrect:* The base pay for a starting worker is determined by their experience and education.

In this example the pronoun ("their") is incorrect because it is plural and the noun ("worker") is singular.

> *Correct:* The base pay for a starting worker is determined by his or her experience and education.

Note: This sentence could be rewritten to avoid the somewhat cumbersome "his or her" wording:

> The base pay for starting workers is determined by their experience and education.

See Chapter 3 for more information on avoiding cumbersome (and sexist) language.

Lack of Parallelism

Parallel construction in sentences can make the difference between communication that is clear and fluid and communication that is awkward and hard to follow. Elements in a series—whether those elements are nouns, verbs, phrases, or clauses—must be parallel (that is, they must match in form) for a sentence to be easily read and understood.

For example, the following sentence is not parallel because the series consists of two nouns ("spelling" and "punctuation") and a clause ("and that the sentence construction is correct"). In a parallel construction, all three items in the series would be either nouns or clauses.

> *Not parallel:* Before final submission, all proposals must be checked for spelling, punctuation, and that the sentence construction is correct.

The sentence should be rewritten as follows:

> *Parallel:* Before final submission, all proposals must be checked for correct spelling, punctuation, and sentence construction.

The next sentence is not parallel because one of the verbs is active and the other is passive.

> *Not parallel:* Anne ordered the new manual, and then the next workshop was planned.

The sentence should be corrected so that both verbs are active:

> *Parallel:* Anne ordered the new manual and then planned the next workshop.

Dangling Modifiers

You might remember the phrase "dangling modifier" as something your teacher wrote on some of your essays—but, like many people, you might never have been really sure what it meant. Perhaps the best way to explain this grammar error is to see it in action.

> *Dangling modifier:* After finally arriving, the banquet began.

If you study this sentence carefully, you will see that the modifier ("After finally arriving") is placed incorrectly because the subject ("the banquet") is not what is arriving. People are arriving. Therefore, the sentence needs to be reworded. Both of the following options work.

> *Correct:* After finally arriving, we joined the rest of our table, and the banquet began.

> *Correct:* After the dignitaries finally arrived, the banquet began.

Note, too, that the subject does not always have to be a person. The following sentence contains some of the same words as the sentence with the dangling modifier, but this sentence is written correctly.

> *Correct:* After finally arriving, the storm caused a power outage, and we could not continue the banquet.

Here the sentence is correct because, in this case, it is "the storm" that "arrived."

The best way to avoid dangling modifiers is to be careful in your writing; reread your written work, check the modifiers, and rewrite the sentences if necessary. Like so many other writing problems, a propensity to dangle modifiers will persist unless you consistently pay attention to the issue.

Key Points of Chapter 2

- When in doubt about how to spell a word, look it up in a dictionary.
- Each punctuation mark serves a specific purpose. Together, punctuation marks tell the reader when to stop or pause, what information belongs together, and what the writer intends each sentence to mean.

> • Become especially familiar with the purposes of the following punctuation marks: the period; comma; semi-colon; colon; question mark; exclamation point; parentheses; brackets; quotation marks; and apostrophe.
> • A sentence is constructed correctly when it expresses a complete thought and contains a subject, a verb, and an ending punctuation mark.
> • Common errors in sentence construction include sentence fragments; run-on sentences; subject-verb disagreement; subject-pronoun disagreement; lack of parallelism; and dangling modifiers. Always double-check your sentences to be sure they do not include any of these errors.

EXERCISES FOR CHAPTER 2

Exercise 2.1

In the following sentences, identify any words that are spelled incorrectly and indicate the correctly spelled word.
   Note: Not all sentences have words with incorrect spellings.

   a. Our training seminar will be complimented by small-group breakout sessions.
   b. Olivia used official stationary to reply to the complaint.
   c. Each employee's evaluation session was enlightning.
   d. Her manager used poor judgement in handling the situation.
   e. Each resident filled out a questionnaire.
   f. Tamara's request was granted; she is being transfered to the Public Works Department.
   g. The mayor renewed her committment to a safer environment.

Exercise 2.2

In the following sentences, add any missing punctuation marks or correct any punctuation marks that are used erroneously.
Note: Not all sentences have missing or incorrect punctuation.

    a. The department heads met for an hour, and then left.
    b. Vehicles with permits can be parked on the street overnight
    c. The library offered the following classes: Excel, Word and Access.
    d. The mayor's top assistant Dan Pavlicek sent the e-mail.
    e. According to the Department of Health, the new ordinance will help "all residents".
    f. The commission referred Mr. Shrader to the proposal which was submitted yesterday.
    g. The new center is scheduled to open its doors tomorrow.

Exercise 2.3

In the following sentences, identify the problem with sentence construction and correct it.
Note: Not all sentences are constructed incorrectly.

    a. The new state law prohibits electronics in landfills, they must be recycled.
    b. A workshop on loans are scheduled for Tuesday.
    c. Flu shots will be offered at grocery stores, pharmacies, and in all park district offices.
    d. Because the emergency plans are ready.
    e. After being ranked a "Top 10 Farmers' Market" in the state, vendor applications for booth space increased.
    f. Either the state or the counties within that state are responsible.
    g. Any senior citizen can apply for their discount.

Answers can be found in Appendix C.

3

Polishing Your Writing

Special Writing Problems in the Public Sector

Knowing the proper mechanics of writing as described in Chapter 2 is a major step toward creating effective writing. Another important step is knowing how to polish your writing. That is, you must work with your writing until it becomes as clear, concise, and coherent as possible.

Expressing yourself clearly, concisely, and coherently is especially challenging in the public sector because people in government agencies have a tendency to write in a legalistic, jargon-filled manner. Some agencies have made efforts to improve their writing as part of the "plain language" movement. For example, in 1998 Vice President Al Gore led a plain language initiative, and in 2010 President Barack Obama signed the Plain Writing Act, which requires federal agencies to write in clear language.[1]

Nevertheless, convoluted writing (often referred to as "bureaucratese") is still the norm in many public agencies. Sir Humphrey Appleby on the BBC television series *Yes Minister* had a humorous way of defining this type of writing:

> Civil Service language: "Sometimes one is forced to consider the possibility that affairs are being conducted in a manner which, all things being considered and making all possible allowances is, not to put too fine a point on it, perhaps not entirely straightforward." Translation: "You are lying."[2]

Expressing yourself clearly, concisely, and coherently in writing is especially critical in the public sector because this sector comprises many audiences, all of whom, with their different backgrounds, interests, and bases of knowledge, must be able to understand—and often quickly respond to or comply with—the information you are communicating.

The steps described below will help you achieve the clarity, conciseness, and coherence in your writing necessary to produce the results you want.

Achieving Clarity

Most of us probably think we already write clearly. After all, we know what we mean, don't we? Getting your reader to know what you mean is not so simple, however. Everyone has a unique frame of reference and will understand and interpret your writing on that basis. Achieving clarity, therefore, requires that you use words that most readers understand and that you use certain writing techniques to ensure that you convey the meaning you intend. The following rules can help.

Rule 1: Use Simple Words

We all like to be regarded as intelligent, and perhaps some of us learned or came to believe that the more syllables our words have, the more intelligent we appear. Actually, though, the opposite is true in most situations. When we use fancy words instead of simple ones, we might not gain the respect of our readers; instead, we may lose their attention and thus fail to achieve the purpose of our message. Therefore, focus on using simple, easy-to-understand words when you write to convey your message quickly and clearly.

> *Original:* Pursuant to our earlier discussion, I will attempt to facilitate the implementation of more collaboration between our departments.

> *Better:* As we discussed yesterday, I will work to improve the communication between our departments.

Original: Our new facilitator brings to the organization years of interfacing with computer networks.

Better: Our new office manager has worked with computers for many years.

The following table lists some formal words and phrases commonly used in the public sector and possible replacements.

Formal Word or Phrase	Suggested Replacement(s)
aggregate	total
commence	begin
discontinue	stop
effectuate	carry out
elucidate	explain
endeavor	try
facilitate	ease, help
finalize	confirm, end
heretofore	previously
implement	carry out, begin
initiate	begin, start
interface	connect
necessitate	need
optimum	best
pursuant to	following
remunerate	pay
reside	live
subsequent to	after
terminate	end, finish
utilize	use

Rule 2: Fix Misplaced Modifiers

When you write your sentences, take care to place any modifying word or phrase next to the part of the sentence it modifies. Otherwise, you will leave the reader confused.

Misplaced modifier: The mayor said on Tuesday she would report on the budget.

This sentence is unclear: did the mayor say this on Tuesday, or is the mayor going to report on Tuesday?

Rewritten: The mayor said she would report on the budget on Tuesday.

Now we know that the mayor will report on Tuesday.

Take care, too, with adverbs to be sure you place them where they convey the intended meaning.

> *Misplaced meaning:* The city council only passed the bill yesterday.

> *Intended meaning:* The city council passed the bill only yesterday.

Hint: Always double-check your sentences for intended meaning when you use limiting modifiers such as "almost," "even," "just," "nearly," and "only."

Other misplaced modifiers can result in unintended humor.

> *Misplaced modifier:* The report was discussed by the board, which had many flaws.
> [The writer might privately think that but most likely did not mean to say it here.]

> *Rewritten:* The report, which had many flaws, was discussed by the board.

> *Or:* The board discussed the report, which had many flaws.

Note: A misplaced modifier is similar to, but not the same as, a dangling modifier. A misplaced modifier is a modifier that needs to be moved closer to the word or words to which it refers. A dangling modifier, on the other hand, is grammatically incorrect because it does not refer in a logical way to any word in the rest of the sentence. See Chapter 2 for our discussion of dangling modifiers.

Rule 3: Avoid Euphemisms

The use of euphemisms—indirect expressions used to avoid being offensive or too harsh (or maybe honest?)—has become a major problem in public sector writing. The effort to avoid being too blunt results not in appreciation for your kindness but in confusion about what you are really trying to say.

Some euphemisms commonly in use today are as follows:

Euphemism(s)	Real Meaning
downsizing, layoffs, reductions in force (RIFs), rightsizing, workforce rationalizations	cuts
revenue augmentation, revenue enhancement, revenue reform	raising taxes
investment	spending
outsourcing	finding cheaper labor elsewhere
defer	will not act
issues	problems
misinformation	lies
less-than-optimal results	failure

If possible, avoid euphemisms—your readers will appreciate the effort.

Rule 4: Avoid Acronyms

Especially in the public sector, it is easy to get caught up in using acronyms (abbreviations made up from the initial letters of terms). Remember, though, that many audiences—especially the general public—might not be familiar with them. If you do use them, be sure to spell them out on first use.

> *Incorrect:* Officials checked the latest EIS when they applied for a CDBG.

> *Correct:* Officials checked the latest environmental impact statement (EIS) when they applied for a community development block grant (CDBG).

Note: Unless you are going to use the term more than once in your message, try not to use the acronym at all.

Rule 5: When Possible, Rewrite Sentences Starting with Expletives

As we mentioned in Chapter 2, in the world of grammar, *expletives* are words or phrases used to fill out a sentence, but they do not, by themselves, add meaning to the sentence. Examples include "It is," "There is," and "There are." A sentence that begins with these filler words can usually be made clearer by eliminating those words and recasting the sentence. Two examples are given below.

Original: There are many problems with this budget analysis.

Better: This budget analysis has many problems.

Original: It is the hope of the trustees that we come to a resolution.

Better: The trustees hope we come to a resolution.

Note: Occasionally, expletive constructions can be helpful. For example, let us say a business owner calls the village manager to report that a neighboring business owner is violating an ordinance by not maintaining his front facade. The village manager might then write a letter to the violator but might not mention the other business owner so as to avoid any personal conflict. The village manager might thus begin his letter by writing, "It has come to our attention that the front of your building is in need of repair." Here the expletive construction is useful.

Achieving Conciseness

In this information age, readers no longer have the time—or the inclination—to wade through wordy writing. To reach your audience, therefore, you need to know how to write concisely, that is, to say everything you need to say in the fewest number of words possible. Such a skill is especially important—and valuable—in the public sector, where overly long and tortuous writing has become the norm. The following rules can help you achieve conciseness in your writing.

Rule 1: Keep Sentences Short

Some people think that the more words they use in their message, the more impressed the reader will be. Just the opposite is true, however. Compare the following examples (the first is quoted directly from a letter written by an attorney).

> *Original:* If we have not assisted you in completing this affidavit in the past, please still feel free to contact me if you have any questions regarding the process, this letter, or would like our assistance in doing the same.
>
> *Better:* If you have any questions or require further assistance, please contact me.

You can sometimes make sentences shorter by eliminating a phrase.

> *Original:* Elaine is the one who went to the manager.
>
> *Better:* Elaine went to the manager.
>
> *Original:* Roberto gave an answer that was clever.
>
> *Better:* Roberto gave a clever answer.

You can also shorten some longer phrases without any loss of meaning.

> *Original:* Water rationing will go into effect due to the fact that we are experiencing a drought.
>
> *Better:* Water rationing will go into effect because we are experiencing a drought.

Note: You can find a list of these longer phrases and their more concise alternatives in Table A.3 in Appendix A.

You can also eliminate qualifying phrases (sometimes called "weasel words"). Eliminating such phrases not only shortens your sentences but also creates sentences with more impact.

> *Original:* It would seem that the meeting was a success.

> *Better:* The meeting was a success.

Other qualifying phrases include "In my opinion," "I think that," "It may be that," and "As best I can surmise." Delete these phrases when you can.

Rule 2: When Possible, Change Verbs from Passive Voice to Active Voice

Like euphemisms, the use of the passive voice in public sector writing has become a problem. Some writers adopt the passive voice to avoid taking or placing responsibility ("Mistakes were made"; "It was decided to move forward with the plan."). Other writers adopt it in an effort to be polite. Much like euphemisms, however, the passive voice can leave readers confused (Who made those mistakes? Who decided to go forward with the plan?). Such writing also lessens the impact of what we are saying, and thus we lose the reader's interest.

Try to get into the habit of using the active voice in your sentences. It not only makes your writing livelier but also usually reduces the number of words you need to express yourself clearly.

> *Original:* The payment made to the vendor was mailed by Susan yesterday.

> *Better:* Susan mailed the payment to the vendor yesterday.

To avoid the passive voice, pay attention to your sentence construction. Have the subject of the sentence appear first, followed by an active verb and then the object of the action.

Note: In some circumstances, the passive voice is preferred. This is generally the case in legal situations in which the law is the actor ("If you do not pay your utility bill, your service will be cut off.") or when you need to emphasize the object of the action ("Any employee who breaks this rule will be disciplined."). In some cases, too, the passive voice may sound less stilted than the active voice, and its presence can add variety and rhythm to your writing.

Rule 3: Eliminate Redundancies

The English language seems to be full of redundancies. The following table lists some redundant phrases and suggested replacements.

Redundancy	Suggested Replacement(s)
absolute necessity	necessity
absolutely complete	complete
actual fact	fact
advance planning	planning
and also	and, also
basic fundamentals	basics, fundamentals
capitol building	capitol (Capitol for U.S. Congress)
close proximity	close, near, in proximity
collaborate together	collaborate
completely unanimous	unanimous
connect together	connect
end result	end, result
exact same	same
fellow coworker	coworker
final completion	completion
free gift	free, gift
honest truth	truth
join together	join
necessary requirement	requirement
new breakthrough	breakthrough
new innovation	innovation
other alternative	alternative
overexaggerate	exaggerate
past history	past, history
personal opinion	opinion
postpone until later	postpone
refer back	refer
repeat again	repeat
return again	return
sum total	sum, total
true fact	fact
usual custom	custom

Rule 4: Eliminate Clichés

Sometimes a writer uses a cliché because it seems to fit the situation, but unfortunately, its use simply tells the reader that the writer could not be bothered to write in a more thoughtful way. Moreover, many clichés are just plain annoying. Here are some to avoid:

at the end of the day (unless you really are referring to the end of the day)

at this point in time

bottom line

empower

get your ducks in a row

going forward

guesstimate

hit the ground running

in the near future

incentivize

interface (as a verb)

leverage (as a verb)

on the same page

optimize

reach out

repurpose

paradigm shift

take it to the next level

think outside the box

win-win

with all due respect

You might think of some, too; feel free to add them to this list.

Rule 5: Be Sure to Use the Correct Word

As we discussed in the Spelling section of Chapter 2, because many words sound alike, it is easy to become confused as to their meaning and then use them incorrectly. For example, one of the most misused sets of words is "effect" and "affect." Although "effect" can be used as either a noun or a verb, it is most often used as a noun. It means the intention, result, or essence of something.

"Affect" can also be used as a noun or a verb, but it is most often used as a verb; it means to act on or influence.

The ruling had an immediate effect.

The judge's action affected all the residents.

We also have other words that, even though they do not sound alike, have nevertheless become confused through frequent misuse. One such set of words often misused these days is "figuratively" and "literally." "Literally" means in an actual sense or exactly, whereas "figuratively" means just the opposite, that is, metaphorically or not literally. Therefore, do not write, "I literally nailed that speech" unless, like Martin Luther, you actually took a hammer and a nail and attached your communication to a door or some other object.

In Table A.4 in Appendix A, we present a glossary of words that are commonly misused. The misuse of words may not always affect understanding, but such carelessness does reflect poorly on the writer.

Rule 6: Eliminate Biased Language

It is important to eliminate biased language. For example, we should avoid the former practice of using the masculine form as a generic term to refer to individuals and groups. Sentences usually can be reworded to eliminate this problem.

Biased: Each resident must pay his fee by April 1.

Reworded: All residents must pay their fee by April 1.

Or: Each resident must pay the fee by April 1.

Or: The fee must be paid by April 1.

Also check your writing to be sure you have not unintentionally stereotyped or offended another person or group. For example, when writing about someone who has an illness or disability, be sure the illness or disability is relevant to what you are writing.

> *Not acceptable:* Patrick, who works in Purchasing and uses a wheelchair, was employee of the month in April.

> *Acceptable:* Patrick, who works in Purchasing, was employee of the month in April.

Note: Attempts to avoid biased language sometimes result in awkwardly worded sentences. For example, some people try to avoid gender bias in the singular pronoun "he" by using "he or she" or "he/she" in their writing. These terms are cumbersome, however, and we recommend rewording. See Table A.5 in Appendix A for a list of some common words and terms that might imply bias and suggested bias-free alternatives.

Achieving Coherence

Writing coherently involves expressing your thoughts in an easy-to-follow manner. That is, whether you are writing an e-mail, a memo, a letter, or other type of communication, your sentences in that message should flow logically, from one to the next, and your paragraphs should do the same. Coherence allows your reader to follow your points easily, thus making your writing effective.

The following guidelines will help you achieve coherent writing:

- Before you begin writing, decide what the main point of your message is and what secondary point(s) you want to include.
- If your message is going to contain more than a few paragraphs, first create an outline of the point(s) you wish to convey. (See Chapter 1, Step 4 for more on outlining.)
- Start your message with a summary of your main purpose for the message.
- Follow this summary by writing, point by point, the message you wish to convey. Each paragraph should start with a general

point, followed by any specific points you wish to include to enforce that general point.

- Use paragraphs to shift from one point to the next.
- Be sure to link the first sentence of each new paragraph with the topic of the previous paragraph. You will then keep your message connected.
- Use transitional words and phrases to create a logical flow. The following are some frequently used transitional words and phrases:
  - To indicate additional information: "also"; "in addition"; "furthermore"; "moreover"; "first . . . second . . . third . . ."; "too"
  - To clarify: "in other words"; "that is"; "in effect"
  - To compare: "likewise"; "in a similar manner"; "also"
  - To contrast: "however"; "nevertheless"; "on the one hand . . . on the other hand"; "still"; "although"; "though"; "yet"; "on the contrary"; "nonetheless"
  - To provide an example: "for example"; "for instance"; "in particular"; "to illustrate"
  - To indicate time: "after"; "before"; "during"; "meanwhile"; "then"; "when"; "while"; "in the meantime"; "in the past"; "in the future"; "later"
  - To indicate place: "above"; "below"; "beside"; "next to"; "around"; "to the left/right"
  - To indicate a result: "therefore"; "so"; "thus"; "hence"; "consequently"; "accordingly"; "as a result"; "as a consequence"; "for that reason"
  - To summarize or conclude: "in sum"; "in summary"; "in conclusion"; "to conclude"; "therefore"; "thus"; "in short"
- Use pronouns to refer to previous nouns. Examples include "he," "she," "it," "they," and "their."
- Repeat key words.
- If you are writing a long document, insert headings to indicate a shift in thought. Be sure, however, that each heading relates to the main topic.

The following example shows coherent writing in action. In this example, the administrator of a school district is describing how the district spent funds on capital projects during the summer of 2014. The administrator decided to report on the projects in chronological order, which was a logical way to present the message. His remaining task was to be sure his sentences flowed smoothly. In the following, we have italicized the words that show the logical flows and transitions.

Example of Coherent Writing

Status of Schoolyard Upgrades—District 47

In accordance with the referendum approved by the voters in April 2014, we completed the planned upgrades at Taft, Wadsworth, and Keats elementary schools during the summer of 2014 and are providing the following status report.

The *first* project, installing a new drainage system and reconfiguring the gas lines at Taft Elementary, began on June 2, 2014. *It* was completed on June 27.

The *second* project, installing new concrete footings at Wadsworth Elementary, was scheduled to start on June 30. The project was delayed, *however*, because of two unforeseen circumstances. *First*, the severe storm of June 29–30 created a delay of two days. *Second*, once we started the work, we discovered a previously unknown gas line, which resulted in us having to do some work by hand. This delay put us behind another two days, and *thus* we were not able to begin the installation of the footings until July 9. *As a result*, we did not finish the project until July 21. *Nevertheless*, because we had anticipated possibly delays, these problems did not delay the start of the third project.

This third project, the installation of new playground equipment at Keats Elementary, started on July 24 and was completed on July 31.

In conclusion, I am pleased to report that all the projects were completed for less than the approved budget estimates. *Moreover,* I will note that our work has helped transform our schoolyards into better learning environments for our children, *thus* keeping the promise we made during the referendum process.

Key Points of Chapter 3

- Being able to express yourself clearly, concisely, and coherently is especially valuable in the public sector because of the varied audiences to be addressed.
- To write clearly, adopt the following habits: use simple words, check for and fix misplaced modifiers, avoid euphemisms, avoid acronyms, and rewrite sentences starting with expletives.
- To write concisely, develop the following habits: keep sentences short; change verbs from passive to active voice (but use passive voice to show the law as the actor, to emphasize the object, or to vary your sentences); eliminate redundancies; avoid clichés; double-check to be sure you used the correct word; and do not use biased language.
- To achieve coherence in your writing, first create an outline of what you want to say. Then, in your first paragraph, summarize the main reason you are writing. Follow this paragraph with paragraphs that back up your main reason. Create a logical flow by using transitional words and phrases throughout your message. Repeat key words as necessary.

EXERCISES FOR CHAPTER 3

Exercise 3.1

Rewrite the following sentences to make them clearer.

    a. The dog owner found a new dog-friendly park for his pet, which was only two blocks away from his house.
    b. The Accounting Department will endeavor to ascertain the amount of remuneration due to the employee.
    c. DHS will hire four hundred more TSA agents by the end of the fiscal year.
    d. The board argued in favor of downsizing the department.
    e. It is the plan of this office to fund next year's Fourth of July parade.
    f. We plan to elucidate the heretofore confusing proposal.

Exercise 3.2

Rewrite the following sentences to make them more concise.

    a. Due to the fact that we are expecting more than five inches of snowfall after 6:00 p.m. tonight, we will implement our snow emergency plan now.
    b. The Andrews family is delighted to live in close proximity to the new school.
    c. With this effort, we can take the village to the next level.
    d. Less people came to the hearing than we expected.
    e. Residents are being urged by city officials to boil their water today.
    f. Local policemen arrived at the scene within minutes of the accident.

Exercise 3.3

Indicate the words in the following paragraph that help the writing achieve coherency.

After the Transportation Committee hearing, many residents remain unhappy with proposed changes to North Street. For example, business owners expressed concern over lost business during the construction period. In addition, residents who live on 16th Street voiced opposition because vehicles would be temporarily rerouted along their street, resulting in increased traffic in a school zone. Nevertheless, the Transportation Committee is set to approve the motion to bring the proposal to the full council.

Answers can be found in Appendix C.

4

Proofreading

The word "proofreading" originally referred to reading a printer's proof pages and marking any errors, but the term has come to mean checking any document to be sure it does not contain any errors in spelling, grammar, or content. This task might seem tedious to some people, but it is critical to achieving effective writing. If you send out a document that has errors, you are telling the reader that you are careless. As a result, both you and your message will lose credibility.

In this chapter we first discuss the proofreading process in general. We then provide a list of the common marks used in proofreading and examples of how to use them.

The Proofreading Process

Proofreading is an acquired skill, and, as with any such skill, it takes practice before you develop an eye for catching all of the errors that can crop up in a document. Proofreading is also a process in that you can develop a series of steps to make the task both more effective and more efficient. The following steps can help you to produce error-free documents:

- Take a break after you have finished writing and before you start proofreading (at least sixty minutes, if possible). It is easy—too easy—to read what you think you wrote; you are much more likely to see errors if you can get away from your writing for a while and then look at it again. Also, if your document is long, take some breaks during the proofreading process—both the brain and the eyes can tire quickly during the task.

Hint: If you do take breaks during proofreading, mark or flag where you left off before setting aside the copy; if you use this method, you will be less likely to start back on the wrong line. When you come back to the document, reread a line or two above where you left off to reduce the likelihood of missing errors in this part of the text.

- Find a quiet place to read. Errors are easy to overlook when you are distracted.
- Although you should not rely only on the spell-checker in your word-processing program, do run it once to catch obvious typographical errors and misspellings.
- Print out a copy of the document (preferably double-spaced for easier reading) and proofread the hard copy. Scientific research has shown that people do not read as well on computer screens as they do on paper—they tend to miss more words and read with less comprehension—so we strongly urge you to follow this step.[1]

    Note: If you are facing a tight deadline and simply do not have the time to print out the document, you can at least take advantage of some of the features of your word-processing program to make proofreading on the computer screen more effective. For example,

    ○ Enlarge the font or use the "zoom" command to make the letters larger and thus easier to read.
    ○ Increase the line spacing to double- or triple-spacing. As noted above, this extra spacing will make the text easier to read.
    ○ Double-check any text you have cut and pasted from an-other document. As you might know firsthand, errors can occur when trying to take shortcuts of this kind.
    ○ Follow the rest of the steps listed in this section.

- Read the document slowly. If you look at every word, you will be more likely to notice if a word is missing, misspelled, or used incorrectly.

    Hint: Some people try to slow themselves down by reading the document backward (from right to left); however, you can still miss errors this way, so if you find this method difficult or uncomfortable, do not use it.

- Read the document out loud to yourself or have another person read the document out loud while you read along silently. With long documents, you might want to change roles halfway through the process.
- Develop a systematic approach to the proofreading process. For example, you might try the following:
  - First read through the document, looking only for errors in spelling and punctuation.

    Note: Remember that spell-checkers will not catch many common typing errors, such as "then" for "than," "it's" for "its," "out" for "our," and so forth, so be alert for these possibilities as you read. You might also find it helpful to review the word listings in Tables A.1 and A.4 in Appendix A before you start proofreading.

  - Read through the document again, looking for errors in grammar and sentence construction. For example, check that all singular subjects have singular verbs and check phrasing to be sure you have not created any dangling modifiers.

  - Read through the document yet again, this time looking for errors in content; that is, check to be sure that you said everything you wanted to say and that you did so in a clear, concise, and coherent manner.

Next, double-check the following specific items:

- *Names:* Be sure all proper names are spelled correctly.
- *Titles:* Be sure all titles are correct.
- *Numbers:* Be sure all numbers, including dates and numbers listed in sequence, are given correctly. Numbers are not only easy to mistype but also easy to misread. When we type or read too quickly, we can easily transpose or skip numbers.
- *Words in all capital letters:* Spell out the letters as you read them; when we proofread a word in all capital letters, we will sometimes not notice that the word is misspelled.

- *Tables:* Proofread with the aid of a ruler. Run the ruler across the page horizontally to be sure all rows align properly, and then check the vertical alignment of the columns to be sure that all numbers and decimal points align properly. Remember, too, to double-check all of the math (for example, double-check that numbers in rows and columns add up to the totals shown).
- *Figures:* Be sure that any labels (for example, names, letters, and numbers on a map) shown on a figure are explained either in a key on the figure or in a caption below the figure.

If you are proofreading typeset copy (for example, page proofs for your next newsletter), also check for the following:

- Incorrect word breaks (incorrect end-of-line hyphenation) can sometimes occur with computerized typesetting programs. For example, be sure that words with more than one meaning are divided correctly ("pres-ent" [noun] versus "pre-sent" [verb]). You might want to make a list of any incorrect word breaks you find so that you can refer to the list the next time you proofread typeset copy.
- If the copy has more than three lines in a row ending in hyphens, circle the area so the typesetter can reset one or more of those lines (having too many hyphens in a row is very distracting to readers).
- Also circle any area where more than three lines in a row end with the same word so that the typesetter can reset one or more of those lines.
- Be sure that special fonts (for example, italic and bold) and symbols (for example, bullets and plus signs) were not changed or dropped in the typesetting process.
- Also check that all paragraphs and other indentations were maintained.
    Note: Other errors can crop up in typeset copy. If you find you are proofreading a lot of material in this form, check more specialized resources (for example, various websites offer tips on proofreading typeset pages).

Below is a sample checklist for proofreading. You might want to personalize this checklist and then make copies to use when proofreading your documents.

Sample Checklist for Proofreading

❐ Spelling and Punctuation
   Words I tend to miss (*examples:* the, an): _____

   _____

   Words I tend to misread (*example:* then): _____

   _____

   Words I tend to misuse (*example:* affect/effect): _____

   _____

   Punctuation I tend to miss (*example:* quotation marks before and after words): _____

   _____

❑ Sentence Construction
   Problems I tend to miss (*examples:* lack of parallelism, dangling modifiers): _____

   _____

❑ Clarity, Conciseness, Coherence
   Problems I tend to miss (*examples:* jargon, misplaced modifiers, missed point in outline): _____

   _____

❑ Proper Names: All names spelled correctly
❑ Titles: All titles correct
❑ Numbers
   ○ Dates correct
   ○ All other numbers correct
❑ Words in Capital Letters: All spelled correctly
❑ Tables
   ○ Title correct
   ○ Rows align
   ○ Columns align
   ○ Math correct
   ○ Other: _____

❑ Figures
   ○ Title correct
   ○ All labels explained either in key on figure or in caption below figure
❑ Typeset Copy
   ○ All word breaks correct
   ○ No more than three line-ending hyphens in a row
   ○ Special fonts okay
   ○ All indents okay

Proofreading Marks

When you proofread your documents and need to indicate changes, you should use universally recognized proofreading marks. These marks, used by writers, editors, printers, and others in the publishing industry, will make your work more efficient. Commonly used proofreading marks are listed below.

Proofreading Mark	Meaning	Example
	Delete	editor
	Close up	per cent
	Delete and close up	proofreading
	Insert	net
	Insert space	thecouncil
	Insert comma	the building which
	Insert period	MD
	Insert quotation marks	Now is the time
	Insert colon	the following
	Insert semicolon	property taxes
	Insert parentheses	August
	Spell out	abbr.
	Insert hyphen	doublespace
	Lowercase capital letter	Mayor
	Uppercase a letter	joseph
	Set in small capital letters	trustee
	Transpose letters	servface
	Start new paragraph	the month. The

Proofreading Mark	*Meaning*	*Example*
‖	Align vertically	45 ‖ 46
⌐	Move left	⌐the message.
⌐	Move right	the message. ⌐
⌐ ⌐	Center	⌐ The Message ⌐
⌐	Start new line	Reading the Proposal
___	Change to italic type	Chicago Tribune
~~	Change to bold type	Note
(rom)	Change to regular type	sector (rom)
(stet)	Let it (the original) stand	political (stet)
' ' ' ' '	Alternate mark for	
	let it (the original) stand	political ' ' ' ' '

Key Points of Chapter 4

- Proofreading is an acquired skill. The more proofreading you do, the more errors you will catch.
- Proofreading is more efficient and effective if you break the process into a series of steps.
- Proofreading is more effective if you take a break after you have finished writing and before you start proof-reading. When you are ready, print out your document (double- or triple-spaced if possible) and move to a quiet area to read.
- Proofreading works best if you adopt a systematic approach. For example, first read the document to check spelling and punctuation. Second, read the document to check grammar and sentence construction. Third, read the document for content. Fourth, double-check specific items that are easily missed.

- A checklist can help you be sure you have covered all the areas where errors can occur.
- The use of the universally recognized proofreading symbols will make proofreading more efficient.

EXERCISE FOR CHAPTER 4

Exercise 4.1

Proofread the following paragraphs and, using proofreading marks, indicate any errors.

FOLLOW US ONTV AND ONLINE

Residents can find out more about village board activties
by tuneing into cable channel 2 to view board meetings live.
meetings are also stream live on www.grovewood.us/boardtv.
The online sight also offers a list of archive meetings so you
can click on a date and watch a passed meeting.
    Fore more information about these meetings or the village
in general; call us at 555-4238. you can also e-mail village@
grovewood.us.

Answers can be found in Appendix C.

Part II

Basic Forms of Writing in the Public Sector
Public Audiences

5

Memos and Letters

As we noted in the introduction, because the public sector addresses so many different audiences, individuals who write for those audiences must be familiar with and able to write both basic and more specialized forms of communication. In this chapter we review in more depth two of the basic forms of writing in the public sector: memos and letters.

Memos

A memo (the shortened form of the word "memorandum") is a written work-related communication that is usually used to correspond with colleagues within the same organization or with business associates with whom one has established a relationship.

As we noted in Chapter 1, memos follow a standard format. The name of the organization and the word "Memo" (or "Memorandum") appear at the top of the page, followed by the "To," "From," "Date," and "Subject" lines. The lines should be completed as follows:

1. In the "To" line, list the full names and titles of the people who either need to take some action or will be directly affected by the contents of the memo.
2. In the "From" line, insert your full name, title, and department.
   Note: Be sure to sign your name or initials after the typed information; your signature acknowledges your approval of the memo's contents.

3. In the "Date" line, put the month, day, and year you are writing the memo. You can use either words or numbers to indicate this information.

4. In the "Subject" line, give a succinct but complete description of the memo's topic.

   Note: In some documents, this line is titled "Re:" (which is an abbreviation for "Regarding" or "Reference").

5. If other people need to know the information in the memo because they are indirectly involved, place their names at the end of the memo (using either "cc: [name and title]" or "pc: [name and title]"). (The term "cc" is short for "carbon copy," which comes from the time when typists used carbon paper to make a copy of a document they were typing; the term "pc" has come to indicate "photocopy." Either term is acceptable to indicate that a copy of the document is being forwarded to the named individual.)

Memos, by their nature, are informal and usually brief. Below is an example.

Example: Typical Memo

Springdale Public Library

Memorandum

To: Tony Martin, Maintenance Supervisor
From: Linda Pentel, Library Administrator
Date: August 25, 2014
Subject: Meeting in Room 203 on August 26, 2014

We are having a trustees' meeting in Room 203 tomorrow at 10:00 a.m. and need two more six-foot tables set up. Please be sure to set them up by 9:00 a.m. tomorrow.

Thanks for your assistance. If you have any questions, please contact me or my assistant, Scott Wise.

cc: Scott Wise, Administrative Assistant

Note: This sample memo is brief, but occasionally you might need to write a lengthier one. No matter the length, however, be sure to follow the preliminary steps described in Chapter 1 to create the most effective memo.

We often write memos to record information that will be kept on file. Because memos are permanent, written records, keep in mind the following points:

- A memo is a work communication, *not* a personal one. Only strictly work-related topics are appropriate for a memo. Note, too, that the tone of the memo can be informal, but it should also be impersonal.
- The "To" and "From" lines in a memo should include not only the individuals' names but also their titles and/or organizational units.
- *Remember that memos belong to the position, not to the person in the position.* When a person leaves a position, the memos remain in the files and may still affect the position.

A final word on memos: You might occasionally need to write what is called a "memo to the file." This type of memo is directed not to another person but rather to a file where you want to keep information for future reference. This type of memo might document an action you took that other staff might find helpful in the future. Below is an example of this type of memo.

Example: Memo to the File

Memo to the File
From: Regina Ford, Administrative Assistant, Water and
          Sewer Department
Date: September 9, 2014
Subject: William Rhodes, Account #1554318

Mr. Rhodes called today to tell us that he thought his August
2014 water bill was too high. I asked if he had experienced any

water leakage in his home, but he said he had not. I told him to follow our recommended test: take down the numbers shown on his water meter, leave the house for a few hours, and, on returning, check the numbers again. If the numbers have changed, he should call us back. He said he would call back if he had any problems.

Letters

As noted earlier, we generally write letters when we want our correspondence to convey a more formal tone. In addition, we usually write letters when we have several points to make and when we are corresponding with people outside our immediate group of colleagues. In the public sector, that outside group of people can vary greatly: for example, we might write letters to individuals in other government agencies, to vendors, or to an individual citizen. Therefore, we must be extremely careful to write well; through our letters we are representing both ourselves and our organization to the outside world.

Topics of letters vary widely, but the general form and appearance of letters do not. Letters are usually written on high-quality paper—a subtle but important way to convey respect to the addressee. Letters are also usually written on the organization's letterhead stationery (which has the organization's full name, address, and contact numbers printed at the top) and follow a standard format. The elements of a formal letter are as follows:

- Date
- Recipient's full name, title, and address
- Subject line (optional)
- Salutation (or greeting)
    Note: Do not use the recipient's first name unless you know the person.
- Body of letter

- Closing (for example, "Sincerely," "Yours truly," or another standard phrase)
- Four blank lines (which you will use to sign your name)
- Your typed name and title
- Names and titles of other people who will be sent a copy of the letter (if applicable); as with a memo, use "cc:" or "pc:" before the names and titles
- Initials of letter writer followed by a colon and initials of person who typed the letter. If you typed the letter yourself, you can omit any initials.
- The abbreviation "Enc." or "Encl.," followed by a colon and the brief title or description of any enclosure(s) (if applicable)

The following example shows a letter written in a standard format. Many organizations will have a format already set up for letters; this particular format is called "full block," meaning that every line starts at the left margin. Other standard formats are the "modified block" and the "semi-block." You can find more information about these formats online or in any general style manual (see, for example, the *Gregg Reference Manual*, by William A. Sabin, which is cited in the annotated bibliography section of this book).

Example: Letter Written in a Standard Format

[Letterhead of Newport Police Department]

June 6, 2014

Mr. Joseph Kessler
Chief, Ridgeland Police Department
4510 South Water Street
Ridgeland, Michigan 46111

Dear Chief Kessler:

I am writing to congratulate you again on being named the new chief of police of Ridgeland. I hope you will enjoy your new position and being a part of the Northwest Suburban Police Association (NSPA).

I am also writing to follow up on the brief conversation we had at last week's NSPA meeting regarding the possibility of sharing a police substation on the Myrick Street boundary between our two communities. The business leaders on my side of that corridor are supportive of the idea, and I understand that many business owners in your community are, too. Would you be available to meet in the next few weeks to discuss this proposal in more detail? When you can, please let me know whether you are interested in meeting and, if so, what time(s) would be most convenient for you. In the meantime, I am enclosing with this letter some materials put together by my staff on the feasibility of creating the substation at 1400 Myrick Street.

Again, congratulations on your new position. I look forward to talking with you soon.

Sincerely,

Robert Ford
Chief, Newport Police Department

RF:jd

Encl.: Preliminary Findings on Proposed Myrick Street Substation

Note: If you look carefully at this letter, you will see that the writer organized it following the structure recommended in Chapter 1 (that is, it has an introduction, a body, and a conclusion).

As we can see from this example, letters, like all correspondence, should be concise and direct. You should succinctly state the purpose of your correspondence and what action you expect or desire. Be sure that your tone is respectful and that you end your letter on a cordial note.

The following are other points to remember when writing letters:

- Use a reader-friendly typeface and type size. Fonts such as Arial and Times New Roman in 12-point size are easier to read than some fancier fonts.
- Single-space each line, with a double space between each paragraph.
- Do not justify the right margin. Right justification can cause extra spaces between words, making the letter more difficult to read.
- If your letter runs over to a second page, place the following three lines at the top of the second page before you continue with the body of the letter:
  - Name of recipient
  - Date
  - Page number

  For example, in the example above, if the letter did run over to a second page, page 2 would begin thus:

  Mr. Joseph Kessler
  June 6, 2014
  Page 2

  This information provides an easy way to match the pages should they become separated.

We conclude this chapter with a reminder of a point we made in Chapter 1: because we work in the public sector, every communication we write, no matter its form (even a memo to the file), is ultimately a public document. We must always craft our correspondence with this fact in mind.

Key Points of Chapter 5

- Memos are used to communicate with work colleagues and other business associates with whom one has established a relationship; they are meant to be informal and brief.

- Memos are usually written on a page with the name of the organization and the word "Memo" or "Memorandum" at the top, followed by the "To," "From," "Date," and "Subject" lines.
- Letters are usually written on an organization's letterhead stationery and include such standard elements as the date; the recipient's full name, title, and address; the greeting; the body; the closing; the signature of the person writing the letter; and the typed name and title of the person writing the letter.
- Memos and letters should always deal with work-related topics, and they should always be seen as belonging to the organization, not the person writing them.
- All memos and letters are public documents.

EXERCISE FOR CHAPTER 5

Exercise 5.1

Assume you are the supervisor of your organization's technical support department. Write a memo to the staff informing them that, effective August 1, each staff member will need to use an individually assigned copier code to use the copy machine. The change is being made so that copying costs can be charged to specific organizational units. The change is also being made to reduce overall copying costs by making everyone more aware of the monthly costs of copying. The individually assigned copier code number will be sent to employees by e-mail on July 31. Add any other information you think is relevant.

Suggested answer can be found in Appendix C.

6

E-Mail

We devote an entire chapter to the subject of electronic mail (e-mail) because this form of writing has become such a popular way to communicate with others. Writing e-mails allows us to communicate more quickly and efficiently than ever before. That is the good news. There are some negative aspects to e-mail, however. That same speed and ease of use have led us (or at least some of us) to write less carefully, resulting in communications that reflect poorly on us—and, equally important, on our agency or organization.

This carelessness shows up not only in such obvious errors as incorrect spelling and punctuation but also in a seeming lack of awareness of the writer's audience and the appropriate tone for that audience. As we have mentioned before, in the public sector our audience can range from a colleague to the media to members of the public. Therefore, because e-mails are so easy to write and send and because every e-mail is ultimately a public document, we need to take special care to check the content and the tone of each e-mail before we click "Send." The following are some basic rules to observe and important features to note.

Basic Rules

Use Proper English

Even though you might be in a hurry to get your message out, and even though an e-mail is a less formal mode of communication than a letter or memo, be sure to follow the guidelines for proper writing that are outlined in Part I of this book. That is, first determine the why, who, which, and how; follow the basic rules of English; polish your writing; and proofread your message before you send it.

Note: The more you follow the guidelines for proper writing, the more habitual such thinking will become, thus speeding up the entire process.

Include a Greeting and Closing

Similar to a letter, an e-mail should include a greeting and a closing. The greeting can be informal (for example, "Hi, Dave") or more formal (for example, "Dear Mr. Markus"), depending on your familiarity with the recipient. The closing can be as simple as "Regards" or "Best." Be sure your contact information follows your name.

Be Aware of Your Audience

When writing your message, be particularly sensitive to both your role and the role of the person (or the roles of the people) to whom you are sending the message. E-mails, perhaps because they are written and read so quickly, seem to be especially susceptible to miscommunication and misinterpretation; this miscommunication and misinterpretation can be exacerbated if the writer of the e-mail does not take into account the different perspectives and interests of the recipient(s).

This problem is beautifully illustrated in a famous article titled "Seven Letters: A Case in Public Management" (which could be easily updated and titled "Seven E-Mails"). In this article, the writer shows how an original communication requesting additional personnel became, through a series of poor communications and misunderstandings, the cause of serious damage to professional and interpersonal relationships within an organization.[1]

Proofread!

Take the time to proofread your message before you send it. In fact, we recommend that you proofread your message *twice* before you send it (see Chapter 4 for more on proofreading techniques). As you might know firsthand, typographical and other common errors seem to crop up more frequently in e-mails than in other forms of writing.

Use a Professional Tone of Voice

Be careful of *tone.* Even though we might use e-mails on very informal occasions (for example, writing a quick reminder to a friend about a lunch date), we must be careful to be more formal in an organizational setting. Be especially careful in the following situations:

- *Humor:* What we might think is humorous could, in an e-mail, come across as sarcastic or insulting to someone else. Equally damaging, it could come across as sexist or racist. As noted earlier, people in the public sector must take special care that their messages are free of possible misinterpretations. It might help to remember that you will probably not get in trouble for *not* sending a joke.
- *Anger:* Never send an e-mail when you are angry. Even though you might feel justified in doing so, sending an angry e-mail is likely to end up causing you future problems. Wait until your anger passes, and then send the message.

For example, a manager frustrated with his assistants might want to send the following e-mail:

From: Steven Lasky
Sent: Thursday, July 10, 2014
To: George Barton, Lisa Masters, Jack Ramsey
Subject: Weekly Budget Sheets

People: Remember to give me your weekly budget sheets
BEFORE I have to ask for them!

Steve

The manager waited until he had his emotions under control, however. He rethought what his main objective was and then wrote the following:

From: Steven Lasky
Sent: Thursday, July 10, 2014
To: George Barton, Lisa Masters, Jack Ramsey
Subject: Weekly Budget Sheets

Dear George, Lisa, and Jack:

I am writing to remind you that I need your weekly budget sheets each Friday morning by 10:00 a.m. I know we are all very busy, so you might want to set a reminder for this task on your e-mail calendar.

If you have any questions, please let me know.

Thanks,
Steve

This time, the manager, by being respectful of the employees' time, offering a solution to the problem, and not showing anger, is much more likely to achieve his objective.

Maintaining a professional tone also includes keeping the following in mind:

- Do not write e-mail messages in all capital letters. Such e-mails come across to the recipient as shouting or screaming.
- Be sparing in your use of jargon and abbreviations (for example, "BTW" for "by the way"), as well as symbols such as emoticons (for example, :-) to indicate a smile). Not everyone appreciates such informality.

Other Important Features of E-Mails

Also note that e-mails tend to have other important features that need to be checked extra carefully.

The "To" Line

Double-check to be sure you are sending the message to the intended recipient(s). Many people, to their embarrassment, have realized too late that their message went to the wrong person.

The "Subject" Line

Keep this line short, but provide enough information so the recipient knows what the e-mail is about. For example, if you need to change the time of a staff meeting, do not type just the words "Staff Meeting" in the subject line, because that could mean many things. Instead, type "Change in Time of Tomorrow's Staff Meeting"; you are much more likely to get the recipients to read the e-mail right away.

Note: Be sparing in your use of designations such as "High Priority." Do not mark something as urgent unless it really is.

Body

As with other correspondence, be concise. In fact, when writing e-mails, we need to try to be even more clear and to the point than we are with other written documents. As we noted in Chapter 4, research has demonstrated that readers miss a lot more when reading text on a computer screen rather than on a piece of paper.[2] Therefore, be brief and concise, and keep the body of the message as simple as possible. That means keeping your message to one or two points (one is preferable) and avoiding any extraneous material, including insertions of different fonts and graphics. Also indicate whether you expect some action in response or whether the e-mail is for the recipient's information only.

Attachments

Take care when sending attachments. Some attachments are very large and can take a long time to download or can even prevent the message from being received. Be sure the recipients want the attachment before you send it.

"Reply" and "Reply All"

Be sure to double-check the names of all the recipients before hitting "Reply All." Sometimes not everyone who initially received a message needs to see your reply. (Indeed, sometimes you do not want them to see your reply.)

Expectation of Privacy

Finally, be aware of the broader issue of privacy when you write and send an e-mail. As we noted in Chapter 1, all government correspondence is subject to access by others under various freedom of information acts, and e-mails are no exception. In fact, even e-mails that you might think are personal could be subject to open records laws.

In a case in Arizona, the state supreme court ruled that a county official could not declare that certain e-mails he had sent from a county computer were personal and thus not subject to the state's open records law. The court said that a trial judge would read the e-mails first and then decide their status. In another court case, an Illinois circuit court ruled that even text messages and e-mails sent and received by some city council members during a council meeting were subject to the state's freedom of information act.

Thus, a good rule to follow is to regard all e-mails, like the other forms of correspondence discussed in this book, as subject to public scrutiny. In addition, remember that even if you delete an e-mail, that message, and all others, could still be saved on your organization's server or another server and could be used as a part of a legal record. In other words, never write an e-mail message that could not be read by everyone—it just might be.

Key Points of Chapter 6

- Always use proper English when writing an e-mail.
- Proofread each e-mail before you send it.
- Check to be sure you are conveying the proper tone—be especially careful about using humor, and never send an e-mail when you are angry.
- Keep in mind that e-mails are always subject to access by others.

EXERCISE FOR CHAPTER 6

Exercise 6.1

Rewrite the following e-mail, keeping in mind the rules discussed in this chapter and in Part I of this book.

From: Miles
Sent: October 8, 2014
To: Joanna and Derek
Subject: Proposal

Say, what's going on with the proposal I sent you last week? As you know, I need feedback on it by tomorrow, I'm meeting with the guys upstairs on Friday.

Also, this is farther down my list of priorities, but what do you know about the talk going around about an upgrade to the software? Between you and me, we are WAY past time for upgrades around here. Better late than never, I guess!

See ya,
Miles

Suggested answer can be found in Appendix C.

7

Media Releases and Public Service Announcements

Similar to private companies, public sector organizations use various specialized forms of communication to get their messages across to the public. Two of the more common forms used are media releases (also known as press releases) and public service announcements (PSAs). For example, a village might write a media release announcing the hiring of a new police chief; a park district might write a PSA to alert local citizens about park safety rules for summer activities. Both forms are useful ways to let citizens know what is going on in their community (and, by extension, how their tax dollars are being spent on their behalf). Both forms, therefore, are effective marketing tools when used properly—that is, when they are targeted to the right audience(s) and written in commonly used formats.

Many public sector organizations are now posting their news items on their websites and other online platforms (Facebook, Twitter, and the like) in addition to (and sometimes instead of) sending formal media releases and PSAs to media outlets. External media outlets such as newspapers, magazines, and wire services are still valuable resources for most public sector organizations, however, so you should understand how to get your news to them efficiently and effectively.

In this chapter we highlight the main features of media releases and PSAs. Check the resources listed in the back of this book, in libraries, and online for more detailed information about these specialized forms of communication.

Media Releases

To write an effective media release, you need to keep in mind that you are actually writing to two different audiences. Even though you ultimately want your message to be seen or heard by the public, you must first get a media outlet to *want* to publish your message. Many media outlets and individual reporters receive hundreds of media releases each week from both private and public organizations. Your job is twofold: to make your release stand out and to make it easy for the outlet to publish it. You can achieve both of these goals by using the proper format for the release and by writing your news clearly and concisely. The following guidelines can help:

1. Many organizations have a preprinted form with their name, address, contact information, and the words "Media Release" or "News Release" at the top of the page. Complete any of this information if needed.
2. Start the release with the words "For Immediate Release" unless you need the outlet to hold the news for some reason. Center these words on the page and put them in bold type.
3. Write an attention-getting headline. The headline should be short but should provide enough information to indicate what the news item is. For example, which of the following do you think both the reporter and readers would be more likely to look at: "Mayor Looks at Budget This Week" or "Mayor Looks to Cut Taxes"? Obviously, the second headline is much better—it really is news, and it is news the public will be interested in following.
4. Write an attention-getting *lead*. The lead (the lead paragraph) should contain any key information on the who, what, where, when, why, and how of the story (in other words, the "5 Ws and 1 H" discussed in Chapter 1).
5. Complete the body of the release with the rest of the details of the story. (If applicable, add a brief description of your organization at the end of the news story.)

6. At the end of the news portion of your release, insert "###," "-30-," or "END." Journalists usually use one of these indicators to signal the end of a news story.

7. If applicable, add the name of the person whom the media outlet should contact to obtain more information. Include the person's telephone number and e-mail address.

Note: Be sure to write the body of the release in what is called the "inverted pyramid" style. In this style, you always place the most newsworthy information first (in the lead), then add important details, and then finish with more general information. Keep in mind that because media outlets have only a limited amount of space (and time), they will sometimes cut the last paragraph or two of a release, so putting the most important information first is vital.

Following is a sample media release:

Example: Press Release for a Local Newspaper

Press Release
Essex Public Library   Contact: Amy Booth
100 Harvard Street   (205) 555-4234
Nomo, AL 35455   abooth@esspl.org
Date: August 19, 2014

FOR IMMEDIATE RELEASE

Library Names New Administrator

The Essex Public Library has named Oscar Guillen the new executive director of the library. He starts on September 2.

"I am honored to be chosen," says Guillen. "I look forward to implementing the vision we all share to make this library *the* resource for all our citizens."

Mr. Guillen, a longtime resident of Essex, was previously assistant executive director at the Woodland Public Library. He also served for seven years as a member of the executive board of the Calumet County Library Association. Guillen received his master's degree in library science from Sangamon University and his bachelor's degree from Bergen College.

"The Library Board feels very fortunate to have Oscar as our new executive director. His ideas to improve customer service and develop our computer resources are indeed exciting," states Mei Tian, president of the Essex Library Board of Trustees.

Guillen replaces Gina Rampel, who retired January 31.

The Essex Public Library, a 2013 winner of the "Most Improved Library" Award, serves a population of 7,400. Its book collection totals more than 15,000 volumes, and it has just opened a new technology center with 18 computers available for public use.

For more information or to schedule an interview with Mr. Guillen, contact Amy Booth, media representative, at (205) 555-4234 or abooth@esspl.org.

Note: Because media releases are sometimes prepared in a hurry, it is easy to make errors. In fact, errors occur so frequently that the wire service BusinessWire tried to help writers by publishing a list of the ten most common errors their editors see. Among the errors they listed were the following: missing or incomplete contact information; incorrect day and/or date; and the incorrect use of words.[1] Be sure you always proofread your media releases before you send them. See Chapter 4 in this book for more information on effective proofreading.

Public Service Announcements

As noted earlier, public service announcements are similar to media releases in that they are used to notify the media about a specific event or service of interest to the public. PSAs, however, generally focus on those events and services that affect the overall welfare of the community. Public organizations use PSAs to inform the public about health and safety issues, community services, and other public affairs. For example, a local government might issue a PSA to inform citizens what steps to take if they hear a tornado siren; another agency might issue a PSA about a new early childhood reading program.

PSAs also differ from media releases in format. They tend to be simpler in structure. For example, you might just use your organization's letterhead, write the announcement, and fax it to a newspaper to request publication. PSAs also differ in that many are written as scripts to be read on the air by a television or radio announcer. Others are produced on CDs, DVDs, or computer files and sent to the various media outlets to play.

Note: Because the Federal Communications Commission requires television and radio stations to serve what it terms "the public interest," and because PSAs are used to meet this requirement, many public agencies are successful in getting their PSAs on the air.

Below is an example of a PSA prepared for airing on the radio.

**Example: Public Service Announcement
Sent to a Local Radio Station**

Milner City Hall
465 Grant Avenue
Milner, Ohio 44444

Public Service Announcement

For Immediate Release
Good Until: July 31, 2014
Contact: Walter Egan
(652) 555-7390
wegan@milner.gov
Duration: 0:30

> Because of the extremely high temperatures we have experienced lately, the City of Milner wants to remind you to keep your pets safe. Never leave your pet alone in a parked car, even with the windows open. Also watch for these warning signs of overheating in pets: difficulty breathing, weakness, trembling, or seizures. Keep pets out of the sun and well hydrated. For more information, call the Milner Animal Services Department at (652) 555-7385 or check the department's website at www.milnercity/animalservices.

Note: Limit your announcement to approximately eighty words for a thirty-second spot.

Other Important Points

You should also keep in mind the following points when writing media releases and public service announcements:

- Stick to the facts. Reporters and other journalists will not accept pieces that contain advertising (subtle or not) for your agency or organization.
- Always double-check your facts before you send your piece.
- Educate yourself on the needs of the media outlet(s) you are contacting. Each has its own requirements for the submission of news items. For example, some outlets now prefer to receive news items by e-mail only.
- Remember that you are much more likely to have your item published if the reporter does not have to make many changes to it before publishing it.
- Some writers recommend that you create your headline *after* you have written the release or announcement. As you write, your ideas and emphasis sometimes change, so writing the headline after writing the body of the text can help ensure that the headline accurately represents the final body copy.
- Quotations add interest, perspective, and legitimacy to a news item, so use one or more of them when possible.

- Some writers suggest limiting releases and announcements to one page; however, some topics in the public sector are inherently complicated (for example, releases containing budget details), so you might need to use more pages to relay the information (but, of course, remain concise with all subjects).
- Some government organizations have their own prepackaged press kits, which include fact sheets and other background information for journalists. Be sure to send one of these kits when the information in it is relevant to your current piece.
- Finally, as stated earlier, check other resources (books, articles, and websites) for more information. Look at previously published media releases and PSAs to get a sense of what types of releases and announcements are most effective.

Key Points of Chapter 7

- Media releases and public service announcements are useful ways to let citizens know what is going on in the community.
- A media release has two audiences: media outlets and the public.
- A media release should always provide the most newsworthy information in the first paragraph.
- Public service announcements tend to focus on information that affects the overall welfare of the community.

EXERCISE FOR CHAPTER 7

Exercise 7.1

In the following press release, using the numbers in front of each paragraph to represent that paragraph, list those numbers to show what the inverted pyramid order is for the release. In other words, arrange the numbers so that the number of the paragraph with the most newsworthy information is first, followed by the number of the paragraph with the next most important details, followed by the number of the paragraph with the next most important details, and so forth, in descending order of importance.

NEWS RELEASE
CITY OF MCGUIN
625 North Forest Street
McGuin, NE 68100
Date: June 24, 2014

FOR IMMEDIATE RELEASE

Free Disposal of Hazardous Waste

[1] Residents can contact Tony Amato in the McGuin Public Works Department for more information on what will and will not be accepted. His telephone number is (611) 555-9823; his e-mail address is tony.amato@mcguin.us.

[2] Accepted household hazardous waste items are as follows:

- automobile antifreeze
- batteries
- cleaning products
- insecticides
- light bulbs (fluorescent and CFLs)
- paints (oil-based only)

[3] On Saturday, July 12, McGuin residents can bring their household hazardous waste to McGuin Park for free disposal. The collection will start at 9:00 a.m. and end at 3:00 p.m. McGuin Park is located at 493 East Second Street.

[4] Items that cannot be accepted include the following:

- business waste
- empty spray cans
- latex paint
- tires

[5] Media should contact Andrea Wilson in the McGuin Communications Department for more information. Call (611) 555-9834 or e-mail awilson@mcguin.us.

[6] Remember that it is illegal to dispose of any hazardous materials in the trash or sewers. Such disposal harms both the environment and anyone who comes into contact with these materials while collecting trash or working on sewers.

Answer can be found in Appendix C.

8

Newsletters

Newsletters are a convenient way for public organizations to provide an array of news and other information to a variety of audiences. Especially with the advent of desktop publishing, newsletters have proliferated, with some public organizations issuing not only community-wide newsletters but also agency-specific ones. For example, a public library might e-mail a biweekly or monthly newsletter to patrons to let them know about the arrival of new books and the details of upcoming events. Other agencies might publish in-house newsletters.

In this chapter we focus primarily on the community-wide newsletter because it is one of the most common types of newsletters used by public organizations. Such newsletters can be an efficient way to inform all citizens about current events in the community. They are also a good way to highlight services and new initiatives, thereby not only communicating news but also increasing awareness of the value of the organization to the public. When newsletters are done well, they can also help create a sense of community among the residents and trust in the organization.

The content, format, design, and frequency of these community-wide newsletters will vary depending on the resources available to cover the costs of collecting, writing, printing, and disseminating the information. Nevertheless, the steps to creating an effective newsletter apply regardless of other variables. To be effective, a newsletter must contain well-written and informative content that is presented in a well-designed format and published on a regular schedule. We provide an overview of these characteristics below.

Content

You can produce a well-written and informative newsletter using the following guidelines.

Grammar

As with any other form of writing, observe all the basic rules of English grammar. In each article you write, check and double-check your spelling, punctuation, and sentence construction; polish your writing so it is clear, concise, and coherent; and proofread what you have written. (See Chapters 2, 3, and 4 for more details on these elements of the writing process.)

Facts

Check and double-check to be sure all the information you are providing is factually correct.

News Text

Remember that you are relating news you want the reader to see and, in some cases, respond to in a timely fashion. Therefore, you need to create text that will attract and keep the reader's attention. The following guidelines will help you achieve that goal:

- Keep the lead paragraph short but provide enough information to invite interest. You do not necessarily need to use the journalist's formula of placing the who, what, where, when, why, and how in the lead (see Chapter 1 for more on this formula), but be sure to use short words and phrases—they are more likely to draw the reader into the article. Some newsletter writers recommend limiting each sentence to no more than twenty words.
- Keep each subsequent paragraph short. Two to three sentences per paragraph is usually adequate.

- Use active verbs, as they help create more attention-getting text and make reading easier for a wide range of people.
- Write each article's headline after you have completed the body of the article. Each headline should be short, while providing enough information to get the reader's attention.

Audience

Keep your audience in mind as you select the topics to be included in the newsletter. Newsletters directed to the general public are more likely to be read when they contain a variety of news and feature articles. The following subjects tend to generate interest; some or all can be used in each issue of the newsletter, depending on its predetermined length:

- New information on a subject or event that will affect many people in the community (for example, a new roadway being built or a major retail store locating in the community)
- Updates on ongoing community projects, including a summary of the progress made thus far and an explanation of any setbacks
- An article on a new service or program about to begin
- Notices of upcoming special events (for example, a Fourth of July parade or a community picnic)
- A feature story on a citizen who contributes to the community in some way
- A feature story on a public employee and his or her contribution to good governance
- An article describing a specific government department and its mission
- Reminders of dates and times for various community-wide events or services (for example, the vehicle sticker fee deadline, the voter registration deadline, or the schedule of hours for the park district's pool)
- Budget and finance news
- A community calendar
- A directory of public departments

Format and Design

Many public organizations establish a set of formatting and design guidelines to be followed in all official publications. For example, an organization might choose to print all its newsletters using the same green color for its name and logo, setting the text in the same typeface, and displaying the text in three columns on each page. Having a preset style guide of this sort is beneficial for several reasons. For example, the person or persons working on the newsletter do not have to spend time re-creating its setup each time the newsletter is scheduled to be published, thus making the process more efficient. Equally important, producing materials in a format that is familiar to the readers provides a consistent context for the material and connotes stability and thus promotes credibility and trust in the contents of the publication.

That being said, certain elements are common to all well-designed publications. We provide a brief overview of these elements here.

Typography

The style and size of the typeface for the newsletter should be chosen on the basis of what will be most readable and inviting to your particular audience. We recommend the following:

- Use a *serif typeface* (serifs are the short lines at the ends of letters) *for the text* of your newsletter. Serif typefaces commonly used for newsletter text include Times New Roman (Times New Roman), Garamond (Garamond), and Century Schoolbook (Century Schoolbook). Most (if not all) of these typefaces are available in general word-processing and desktop publishing programs.
- Use a *sans serif typeface* (the letters do not have serifs) *for headlines, headings and subheadings, and other display material.* Sans serif typefaces commonly used in newsletters are Helvetica (Helvetica), Arial (Arial), and Futura (Futura).

(These typefaces are also available in most general word-processing and desktop publishing programs.)

Note: Do not mix too many typefaces in the newsletter, as this will distract the reader. Usually, the combination of one serif typeface and one sans serif typeface works well.

Layout and Design

As with the typography, keep the overall look of your newsletter simple and clean. You can achieve this look by using some standard layout and design elements, including the following:

- Create columns (either two or three) of text on each page. Breaking the text into two or more columns generally makes your content look more inviting.
- Place the most important article(s) in the top-left and lower-right sections of the first page. (Reader's eyes tend to start at the upper left and follow the text to the right and then down.)
- Use white space to separate your articles and to create a sense of openness and readability.
- Use what is called a "ragged right" margin; that is, do not justify the right sides of the articles. Full-line justification can make reading more difficult.
- Use headings, subheadings, rules (lines), and text boxes (boxes you insert to highlight particular parts of the text or to add information) to break up the text.
- Again, using one serif typeface for the text and one sans serif typeface for the headlines works well.
- Set the headlines in bold (or bold italic) and make them two sizes larger than the text size. For example, if you use 12-point Times New Roman for your text, you might use 14-point Arial in bold for your headlines.
- Use illustrations (photographs, charts, and graphs, for example) to add visual and contextual interest.

- Be careful not to overuse decorative type ("dingbats"), such as bullets, arrows, and pointing fingers. They quickly become distracting. If necessary to highlight specific points, use bulleted or numbered lists instead.
- Do not overuse color. A newsletter with two colors (usually black and one other color) is not only visually pleasing but also much more economical to produce than more colorful documents (for example, four-color brochures).

See Figure 8.1 (next page) for an example of a well-written and well-designed newsletter.

Publication Schedule

One question remains: Should you publish your newsletter weekly, biweekly, monthly, or at some other interval? The answer to this question will depend largely on the size of your community and the size of the budget allocated for publishing the newsletter. Most newsletters of the type we discuss here are published either monthly or quarterly. Generally speaking, the larger the government, the more often you should publish your newsletter. A good guideline is to check with other communities about your size and see how often they publish their newsletter. Remember, though, that no matter what schedule you choose, be sure to stick to it. The success of this form of communication lies not only in its content and look but also in its dependability.

Also check other communities' newsletters to help you decide how many articles to include in each newsletter. Check with local printers regarding paper and printing costs to find the most efficient way to produce your newsletter.

Note: As with media releases (see Chapter 7), many public organizations now publish their newsletters on their websites, although most public entities continue to mail out a printed version as well. We recommend this practice, but if you find that you simply do not have the budget for printing costs, an online-only newsletter is still a good way to keep the public informed and to create a sense of community and trust in the organization.

Figure 8.1   **Example of Community-Wide Newsletter**

SEPTEMBER 2013 **OP/FYI**

A NEWSLETTER
FROM THE
VILLAGE OF
OAK PARK

VOLUME 25 • ISSUE 7

Residents urged to participate in community survey

Surveys soon will be showing up in the mailboxes of Oak Parkers selected at random to help the Village gauge citizen views on a wide range of community aspects and issues.

While taking only about 15 minutes to complete, the surveys will help policy makers better understand priorities for government action and citizen opinions on quality of life and public services.

Oak Park residents who receive a survey are urged to promptly complete

and return the document to ensure their viewpoints are part of the final tabulation.

About 1,200 responses are needed for a 95 percent confidence level. Survey respondents will remain anonymous.

Officials say residents who are willing to take the time to complete and return the survey will be doing a great service for the community, since the survey results will provide important information for planning how best to allocate municipal resources in the future.

National Research Center, Inc. (NRC), a social science research firm whose core business is community surveys, was hired to ensure the scientific validity of the survey results. NRC assisted with surveys conducted in Oak Park in 2000, 2004, 2008 and 2011.

Results of these past surveys are posted online at **oak-park.us** — just search for community surveys.

Through its collaboration with the International City Managers Association, NRC has developed a national database of community surveys and survey questions, which allow the Village to compare many of the results with those from similar communities in Illinois and across the country.

Surveys in 2000 and 2004 were conducted by telephone. But with telephone response rates plummeting across the industry and costs rising, mail has proven to be a more cost-effective approach.

In addition, officials say mail responses tend to be more candid than those gathered by a telephone interviewer.

For more information about the survey, call 708.358.5791 or email **village@oak-park.us**.

Village launches new website

After months of development, testing and feedback, the new Village of Oak Park website is online. The new site brings a more modern look and enhanced navigation to **oak-park.us**, which had relied on the same design for more than a decade. Users will find much of the same information from the old site, but organized in a more intuitive manner and with an improved search feature. The new website also is a step toward responsive design for better display on mobile devices, which are proving increasingly popular.

All of the familiar, essential online services are available through the new site, including tools to contest and pay tickets, pay water bills and renew vehicle stickers. Much of the old site's archival content will be migrated to the new site in the coming weeks and months. The site displays best in Chrome, Firefox and Safari, but is compatible with Internet Explorer 8 and later versions. Users relying on older versions of IE are urged to update their browsers or install one of the other free browsers. The site was developed

by Breakthrough Technologies, an Evanston-based firm chosen via a competitive bid. For more information on the new website or to provide feedback, email **vopnews@ oak-park.us**.

Source: Courtesy of the Village of Oak Park, Illinois.

In this chapter we have described the basic characteristics of a well-written and well-designed newsletter. If you are responsible for writing and publishing a regular newsletter, you should consider pursuing further information on all of the steps involved in the process. The general field of publishing is a dynamic one; for example, designers continually experiment with new typography, and specialists in the printing industry continue to develop new and more efficient equipment and methods of printing. Be sure to check resources in the library and online to obtain more information on producing effective newsletters. Also consider taking a class or two in graphic design and printing methods; many community colleges offer both individual classes and semester-long programs.

Key Points of Chapter 8

- Newsletters are a convenient way to help public organizations disseminate information and promote the value of and sense of trust in the organization.
- Newsletters should feature timely, well-written, concise articles of interest to a range of people.
- Newsletters should contain a variety of news and feature articles.
- Preset formats and designs create a sense of credibility and trust in the organization.
- Newsletters should be published on a regular schedule.

EXERCISE FOR CHAPTER 8

Exercise 8.1

Locate three community-wide newsletters, read them carefully, and then answer the following questions:

  a. How do the newsletters' appearances differ? In other words, what do you see that differs in the newsletters when you first look at them?

b. How do the articles compare in respect to the quality of writing? For example, are the mechanics correct, and is the writing polished? (See Chapters 2 and 3 in this book for more information on these aspects of writing.)

c. What types of articles does each of the newsletters include?

d. What is the approximate balance among news, feature articles, and other information?

e. Do the stories themselves attract your attention? Why or why not?

f. Which newsletter is the best? Why is it the best?

Suggested answers can be found in Appendix C.

Part III

Basic Forms of Writing in the Public Sector
Internal and Technical Audiences

9

Formal Reports

When it comes to the topic of writing formal reports, we are re-
minded of what Gene Fowler, a journalist and biographer, said
about writing: "Writing is easy. All you do is stare at a blank sheet
of paper until drops of blood form on your forehead."[1] In truth,
writing a formal report will not draw blood, but it does present
some challenges not found in other forms of writing.

To write a formal report effectively, you should, of course, first
follow the preliminary steps we discuss in Chapter 1 and observe
the rules of good writing we describe in Chapters 2 and 3. In addition, though, because a formal report can be complicated in both
its content and form, you need to pay special attention to how you
plan the report and how you write the report. Each of these steps
is discussed in more detail below.

Note: We use the term "formal report" here to refer to a range of
public sector reports—for example, analytical reports, information
reports, planning reports, and research reports, just to name a few.
Note, however, that in this chapter we distinguish reports from
proposals, which can look similar to reports. Because proposals
have key differences from what we refer to here as "reports"—most
notable, perhaps, is that the primary goal of reports is to inform,
whereas the primary goal of proposals is to persuade—we provide
information on proposals in separate chapters. See Chapters 10,
11, and 12 for more information on proposals in general and on
specific types of proposals.

Planning a Formal Report

Like any piece of good writing, an effective formal report requires that you first spend time planning it. Planning this type of report involves three steps: defining the topic, conducting research on that topic, and creating an outline from that research. Each of these steps is described in turn.

Defining the Topic

Even though a variety of formal reports exist, each of them, to be effective, has to begin with someone defining the topic that is to be discussed. (We note here that some report topics are inherently limited; for example, an annual report on water usage in a village is necessarily focused on the topic of water and its usage in a specific area within a specific period of time. Most topics are not inherently limited, however.)

Defining a topic can be something of an art form: it involves making the topic narrow enough so that the report is focused but broad enough so that it covers the subject matter adequately. To define a topic, we find the following process helpful.

1. Conduct some preliminary research on the general topic. For example, pick out some key words on the topic and use these words to look in libraries and online for more information on the subject.
2. Start writing down ideas on how you can approach the topic. Write down answers to such questions as the following:
   a. How much information is available on this topic?
   b. What important issues arise from this topic?
   c. From what angle(s) can I approach this topic?
   d. Do I have any other restrictions to take into account (for example, limited time, a limited number of pages that can be written)?
3. With this information, develop a topic sentence. The topic sentence should answer this important question: *What is the purpose of this report?*

For example, say that you work in the Department of Economic Development in your city, and your supervisor has asked you to prepare a ten- to fifteen-page report on economic trends in the real estate market in the city. Using the questions listed above (2a–2d), you conduct some preliminary research and find the following information:

- Numerous data are available on economic indicators related to local real estate. In fact, you find so much data that you need to limit your topic to a more manageable scope to fit a ten- to fifteen-page report.
- You know from meetings you have attended and reports you have read that the state of the housing market is of great concern to city leaders and the public. Therefore, you decide to focus your report on recent economic trends in the housing market and how those trends relate to those in the real estate market as a whole.
- You create a preliminary topic sentence: "The purpose of this report is to provide information on recent economic trends in our housing market and how those trends relate directly to the city's broader real estate market."

Note that you could have chosen a completely different approach to your report. For example, after conducting your preliminary research, let us say that you found what you thought was significant information on another sector of the real estate market (for example, office space), so you decided to direct your topic to this subject. The important point here is that you narrowed your focus to a manageable topic.

Conducting Research

Now that you have created your topic sentence, you need to conduct more in-depth research to find out what concerns are most relevant to your defined topic. In other words, you need to narrow your focus a second time. This time, take your defined topic, research the main elements that pertain to this topic, and then choose up to three of those elements to discuss in your report.

For example, in the scenario provided above, when you research economic indicators related to recent trends in the city's housing market, you might look at the following three indicators: the number of construction permits, the number of residential sales, and the number of foreclosures. (Again, note that you could have discussed other indicators; perhaps the three given here were the most politically relevant at the time of your report.) You also begin to develop notes on the relationship of these indicators of trends in the housing market to trends in other sectors of the real estate market.

You can research issues related to your topic by looking at both primary and secondary sources. Primary sources are original records created during the time being studied. For example, primary sources for the scenario described here might include local records of construction permits issued, residential real estate transfers, and court records on foreclosures of residential properties. Secondary sources are records created by people who are once-removed from the event(s) being studied. For example, in our scenario, secondary sources might include books and journal articles written by experts who have conducted research on recent regional trends in the housing market and the relationship of those trends to other economic trends.

Note: As you conduct your research and start developing the content for your report, be especially careful to *avoid plagiarism.* Plagiarism can be defined as presenting someone else's words or ideas as your own. To avoid plagiarizing, be aware of the following: (1) when you use another person's exact word or words, you need to place the word or words in quotation marks and cite the source (for more information on how to create citations, see the next section); and (2) when you paraphrase another person's idea or ideas (for example, a specific point, a method, or a conclusion) not considered part of common knowledge, you need to cite the source. ("Common knowledge" can be defined as factual knowledge known either broadly or within your particular discipline. For example, you do not need to document the statement that Ronald

Reagan was elected president in 1980. If you stated, however, that Ronald Reagan helped end the Cold War, you would need to cite the source or sources from which you derived this conclusion.) The best advice: When in doubt, cite the source.

Creating an Outline

You are now ready to create an outline of how you want to present your findings. Refer to Step 4 in Chapter 1 for guidelines on creating an outline.

Writing a Formal Report

Now that you have defined your topic, conducted your research, and created your outline, you are ready to write the report and prepare it for submission. The components of a formal report can vary depending on the organization's requirements, but many reports of this kind contain the following: a title page; a table of contents; an abstract or summary; the text of the report; appendixes (if necessary); a list of notes; and a bibliography or list of references. Each is described in turn below.

Title Page

The title page contains the following: the title of the report, the name of the person or unit to whom the report is addressed, the author of the report (or the name of the department from which the report is being issued), and the date of the report.

Note: Be sure the title is succinct but provides enough information to tell readers what the report is about. For example, in the scenario we described earlier (that is, writing a report on a city's economic indicators in real estate), a title such as "Recent Economic Indicators in Real Estate" would not be as informative as "Economic Indicators in Real Estate: Recent Trends in the Housing Market, 2012–2014."

Table of Contents

In the table of contents, list the chapter titles (if applicable) and the first-level headings exactly as they appear in your report. Place the starting page number of each section to the right of the titles and headings.

Abstract or Summary

Not every report requires an abstract or summary, but if yours does, you should use this section to summarize the main ideas and recommendations (if any) in the report.

Note: Many writers write the abstract or summary after they have completed the main text because ideas and recommendations can change as a report is being written.

Text of the Report

The text of your report, as you might remember from Chapter 1 of this book (and from the outline you prepared in planning your report), should contain three parts: the introduction, the body, and the conclusion. We briefly review these parts below.

The Introduction

In the introduction, include the following: the purpose of the report, the scope (and limitations, if applicable) of the report, the definitions of any key terms, and an overview of what you are going to discuss in the body of the report. Depending on the subject, you might also want to mention briefly such topics as the background of the issues surrounding the topic and the methods you used to conduct your research and analysis.

For example, in the scenario provided above, you could write the following introduction:

The purpose of this report is to provide information on recent economic trends in our housing market and discuss how those trends relate to the city's real estate market as a whole. The report will first focus on three key economic indicators: the number of construction permits, the number of residential sales, and the number of foreclosures. The report will then present researchers' analyses of how these three key indicators reflect trends in the real estate market as a whole.

The Body

In the body of the report, include all the main ideas you want to present. For example, in this section you might define terms; explain where the data came from (sources or data gathering); present and discuss the results; and discuss the implications of the results.

Divide the report into sections (and subsections if the sections are long), insert headings for each section, and put in subheadings for each subsection. These headings and subheadings will make the text more readable and coherent. (See especially the section on achieving coherence in Chapter 3 of this book for ways to create coherence in your sentences and paragraphs.)

The Conclusion

In the conclusion, summarize the main ideas in the report and, if applicable, present any recommendations you wish to make.

Appendixes

Use appendixes to provide any peripheral information, such as data tables and other supporting information for points made in the report.

Notes

You can use notes for two purposes: (1) to add information that you think is valuable for the reader to know but that does not fit well in the main text itself, and (2) to add sources for documents and other materials you quoted or cited in the main text.

Place notes either as footnotes (at the bottom of the page where the note number is referenced) or as endnotes (at the end of the document, after the main text and appendixes but before the bibliography or list of references).

Note: In some documentation styles, you would not use notes to cite your sources. Instead, you would insert information on your sources in the text itself. These types of notes are usually referred to as "in-text citations" or "parenthetical citations." Several style manuals, including the *Publication Manual of the American Psychological Association* (currently in its sixth edition) and the *MLA Handbook for Writers of Research Papers* (currently in its seventh edition), recommend this form of citation. Others, such as the *Chicago Manual of Style* (currently in its sixteenth edition), show both the note form and the in-text citation form. Writers in the social sciences tend to use either the note form of documentation shown in the *Chicago Manual of Style* (known as Chicago style) or the in-text citation format recommended by the *Publication Manual of the American Psychological Association* (known as APA style). No matter which style you adopt, you need to use it *consistently* throughout both your notes and other reference materials. Appendix B in this book provides examples of the documentation styles in the Chicago and APA manuals.

Bibliography or References

A bibliography is an alphabetical list of all the works you consulted to write your report. A references section (or "Works Cited" section) is an alphabetical list of all the works you cited in the text. The form you use will depend on the documentation style you have chosen for your report. Again, see Appendix B for more information on these styles.

Other Important Points

Other important points you should keep in mind as you plan and write your reports include the following:

- The tone of a formal report should be formal; that is, the tone should be objective and impersonal (for example, do not use "you" and "I" in the report).
- Be aware of any political situation that might surround the topic of your report. Present facts and options fairly and do not get involved in office politics. Leave any final conclusions to others (for example, decision makers).[2]
- Appearances are important; prepare your report on good quality paper, and be sure the printing is clear and easy to read.
- As always, proofread your report before you submit it. See Chapter 4 in this book for more on the importance of proofreading and on ways to proofread effectively.

Key Points of Chapter 9

- Effective reports require careful planning and careful writing.
- Planning a report has three steps: defining the topic, conducting research on that topic, and creating an outline.
- When preparing a report, a writer must be careful not to plagiarize. Be sure to give credit for other people's words and ideas.
- Components of a report might include a title page; a table of contents; an abstract or summary; the text of the report; appendixes; notes; and a bibliography or list of references.
- The text of a report needs to have an introduction, a body, and a conclusion.
- All sources must be documented in the same style.

EXERCISE FOR CHAPTER 9

Exercise 9.1

Your supervisor has asked you to clean up a poorly written report (shown below). After reading it, you realize that your first step is to reorganize the report by placing each sentence into one of the following four categories:

- Introduction
- Body
- Conclusion
- Not to be included (no relevant information)

On a sheet of paper, first list the categories. Then, using the numbers shown in front of each sentence in the report, place each number in the proper category.

Red Light Camera Report

[1] Traffic control has been an issue since the Egyptians built the pyramids. [2] Imagine those big stone blocks colliding. [3] Red-light cameras are a modern answer for traffic control. [4] People get hurt in traffic accidents. [5] We should use red-light cameras in our city. [6] They save lives, prevent injuries, and protect property. [7] I know a guy who works for one of those companies. [8] Maybe we should see if they are interested in providing their services. [9] Red-light cameras take a picture of the car's license plate when a car runs a red light. [10] The red-light camera company sends the car owner a ticket. [11] Those tickets are hard to get out of because of the picture. [12] Analysis of accidents suggests that 320 crashes at intersections occurred because vehicles ran red lights. [13] They can tell because the vehicles crash at an angle. [14] Everybody has an angle, I guess. [15] It is just not safe out there. [16] Of course, people will say we are just doing it for the money. [17] Well, there is a lot of money in them. [18] A lot. [19] I hope this is what you wanted.

Answers can be found in Appendix C.

10

Proposals

An Overview

In Chapter 1 we note that, generally speaking, the purpose of a message is to either inform or persuade. When we write a proposal, we focus on the latter purpose; that is, when we write a proposal, we try to persuade another person (or people) to take a particular action or adopt a certain point of view. In the proposal, we describe the problem or opportunity we see, and then we explain how our idea or plan can solve that problem or respond positively to that opportunity. This chapter applies generally to writing all kinds of proposals; the next two chapters discuss, respectively, writing grant proposals and budget justifications, which are two common and important specialized forms of proposals with unique features.

Proposals can be categorized as either informal or formal. Informal proposals are usually sent to other people within one's own department or agency. Formal proposals, though sometimes sent to people in the same department or agency (and usually directed to upper-level managers), are most often sent to people in another organization. The other major differences between the two kinds of proposals are described below.

Note, however, that no matter which kind of proposal you are writing, you need to follow all the basic rules of good writing to make your proposal effective. We recommend that you review the chapters in Part I of this book before and as you write proposals. Pay special attention to the following:

- *Audience:* Know who your audience is. For example, formal proposals are often reviewed by decision makers and experts, so writers must address both the big picture (of interest to decision makers) and the technical details (of interest to the experts). Moreover, any specialized terms will need to be explained because even though the experts might be familiar with these terms, the decision makers might not be.
- *Preparation:* Because proposals can be complicated pieces of writing, spend extra time preparing them. Remember to brainstorm, organize, and write—in that order.
- *Basics of English*: Double-check your writing to be sure you have spelled, punctuated, and constructed your sentences correctly. Errors in these areas will lead to a loss in the credibility of the proposal writer.
- *Polished writing:* Double-check to be sure your writing is clear, concise, and coherent. Readers of proposals are usually very busy, so brevity and logic are critical.

Informal Proposals

As the name implies, informal proposals tend to be less structured than formal ones. Informal proposals also tend to be very brief (from a few paragraphs to a page or two). They describe a relatively simple problem and propose one or more solutions. Informal proposals can be personal in tone (for example, writers might use the personal pronouns "I" and "you" when writing), and they are usually transmitted informally, that is, by e-mail or memo.

To be effective, an informal proposal should be written as follows:

- *Introduction:* Briefly state why you are writing the proposal. Include a description of what the problem is, what you are proposing to do about it, what it will cost, and what the benefit(s) will be.
- *Body:* Provide more detail about the problem and the proposed solution(s). Explain why the problem exists and how your pro-

posal solves the problem. Also describe what specific evidence you have regarding the costs of the problem and the costs and benefits of the solution(s). Provide any cost breakdowns, including details about any personnel and/or materials needed. Attach a timetable if applicable.

* *Conclusion:* Restate the problem and the overall benefits of the solution(s). Include a list of attached supporting documents (if any).

Below is an example of an informal proposal.

Example: Informal Proposal

Memorandum

To: Olivia Menendez, Manager, Accounting Department
From: Jan Olsen, Supervisor, Accounts Payable
Date: May 28, 2014
Subject: Accounts Payable Backlog

As we discussed yesterday, we are starting to experience the same problem in the Accounts Payable Department that we did last year at this time, namely, a backlog in the processing of payments. The backlog results primarily from the increase in the number of people who are paying various fees due at this time of year (annual vehicle sticker fees, pool passes, and park fees, for example). To solve this problem, I propose that we hire a part-time, temporary accounts payable clerk to assist with the processing. I have calculated that hiring this clerk would cost $2,500 (25 hours a week for 10 weeks at $10/hour), but the benefits—faster processing of payments, a reduction in errors, and increased citizen goodwill—will be very worthwhile, as described below.

First, with regard to processing, having an additional staff member will enable the department to get checks to the bank more quickly. As you might remember, last year the department was sometimes three to four days behind in making deposits.

Speeding up the deposits will result in the additional interest of several hundred dollars (see attached calculation sheet).

Second, having an additional staff member would alleviate some of the stress on the current staff, which, in turn, would help decrease the number of errors that naturally occur when trying to go too fast. The Village of Burrwell, which a few years ago experienced this same problem, found that they had 5 percent fewer errors after hiring an extra staff person, and they calculated that they saved several hundred dollars because they did not have to spend the time or money to fix those errors.

Third, having the additional assistance will help reduce the amount of time that people have to wait in line to pay, which, in turn, will improve goodwill. Of course, we cannot put a numeric price on goodwill, but as we both know from our study of public relations, having it is extremely valuable—and losing it, as we found out last year, is extremely costly.

Attached is the interest calculation sheet mentioned above. Given that we still have money left in our personnel line this fiscal year, and given the benefits listed above, I respectfully request permission to start the hiring process for a part-time, temporary clerk.

Formal Proposals

Formal proposals differ from informal proposals in that they describe problems and solutions that are broader in scope. As a result, formal proposals are generally longer and more structured than informal proposals. They also usually require the writer to conduct more research before actually sitting down and preparing them. Formal proposals are also usually intended for a broader audience, so the writer must be especially careful to use impersonal and objective language throughout the document.

Most formal proposals contain several sections (and, depending on the topic, subsections) so readers can more easily follow the description of the problem and the solution(s). Some formal proposals are prepared in response to a request for proposal (RFP), a formal document issued by an agency or organization that describes a need and asks for proposed solutions. If you are responding to an RFP, be sure to follow all the guidelines specified in the request.

Each RFP will be unique, and thus responses will be unique, but generally, most formal proposals contain three main parts: front materials, the body, and the back materials. Front materials usually include a cover letter or memo; a title page; an executive summary; a table of contents; and a list of illustrations. The body usually includes, in some form, a formal statement of the problem or issue; a discussion of alternate solutions; a discussion of the proposal being made; a budget analysis; and the concluding remarks and recommendation(s). Back materials include the appendix(es) and list of references. Each is described in turn below.

1. Cover Letter or Memo

On this page (also called a transmittal letter), include the following:

- A brief description of the document being transmitted (for example, "Enclosed is the proposal on [the project]")
- A brief description of the need and the recommended solution(s)
- A closing sentence that thanks the receiver for the opportunity to submit the proposal and invites a follow-up discussion

2. Title Page

Include the following information:

- The title of the proposal
- Name(s) and title(s) of intended reader(s)
- Your name and organization
- The date of the proposal

3. Executive Summary

The executive summary is a brief synopsis of the proposal. Some executives and other decision makers may read only this section (hence the title) and glance at the rest of the document, so be sure this section is succinct (one page if possible). Include the following information in the executive summary:

- A brief account of the background of the problem and the purpose of the proposal
- The recommended solution(s)
- Any other recommended action(s)

4. Table of Contents

Include the following information:

- A list of all section and subsection titles on left side of page (the subsections should be indented a few spaces in from the left margin); be sure to follow the same numbering system as used in the proposal itself
- The corresponding page numbers on the right side of the page

5. List of Illustrations (if applicable)

List figure and table titles, as well as the titles of other illustrations (for example, maps, drawings, and photographs) and their corresponding page numbers.

6. Statement of Problem or Issue

Include the following information:

- A general description of what problem or issue exists, including any background information on it

- Evidence of the problem or issue
- Documentation of the magnitude of the problem or issue
- Description of any formal policy changes that might be required to solve the problem or respond to the issue; include any changes in laws, rules, or regulations

7. Discussion of Alternate Solutions

This section should discuss all *reasonable* alternate solutions (that is, do not include any false choices or present any choices unfairly) and then describe the preferred solution. Include the following in support of the preferred solution:

- Authority or evaluative standards used to determine that the preferred solution is the best (for example, laws, public opinion polls, ethical standards)
- Evidence that these authorities and/or standards support the preferred solution
- Documentation of any assumptions

8. Discussion of Proposal

Now that you have stated and briefly described the preferred solution, provide a detailed account of the proposal. Include the following:

- What specific action(s) is proposed
- When that action(s) will take place
- Who will act (for example, an organization, subunit[s], or personnel types) and, if applicable, what authority they have to act
- The specific policy changes (for example, laws, rules, or regulations) that will be required

9. Budget Analysis

Explain all costs, and categorize and explain all operating expenses. Be specific with regard to figures and percentages.

10. Conclusion and Recommendations

Summarize the main points, highlighting all benefits that will occur if the proposal is accepted. Place the most important recommendation first.

11. Appendixes (if any)

Include any supporting materials referred to in the proposal.

12. References

List the full citations for any sources cited in the proposal. As noted in Chapter 9, be sure to use one documentation style (for example, the *Chicago Manual of Style*, the *Publication Manual of the American Psychological Association*, or the *MLA Handbook for Writers of Research Papers*). See the annotated bibliography in the back of this book for more information on these resources.

Because of space constraints, we cannot provide an example of a typical formal proposal here. You can access many proposals through various states' websites and through the *Federal Register*'s website (www.federalregister.gov).

Other Important Points

We end this chapter with a few reminders:

- Remember that, by their nature, proposals are challenges to the status quo and thus might be resisted by people instinctively reluctant to change. Reread your proposal before sending it to be sure your arguments are clear and follow a logical pattern. Readers are more likely to be persuaded if they can understand the connections and see the relationships between ideas.

- Proposals, whether informal or formal, should emphasize facts and minimize expression of opinions. Opinions can be easily dismissed or distorted; facts are not as easy to dismiss or distort.
- Check and double-check all your facts. Some readers could discount the entire proposal if even one factual error is found.
- Avoid any temptation to slant or manipulate facts. The costs of doing so far outweigh any benefits, in either the short term or the long term. Once readers discover such dishonesty, both the current proposal and any future proposals will be dismissed.
- Check and double-check all your figures. As with other facts, if the numbers are wrong, the whole proposal will become suspect.
- In your proposal, do not overpromise in terms of what you can actually deliver.

Key Points of Chapter 10

- Proposals can be categorized as either informal or formal.
- Informal proposals tend to be brief and can be personal in tone.
- Formal proposals are more structured than informal proposals and are impersonal in tone.
- Formal proposals usually contain a cover letter or memo; a title page; an executive summary; a table of contents; a statement of the problem or issue; a discussion of alternate solutions; a discussion of the proposed solution(s); a budget analysis; concluding remarks and recommendation(s); appendixes; and references.

EXERCISES FOR CHAPTER 10

Exercise 10.1

You notice that people in your organization frequently complain about the time it takes to get to work and about how hard it is to schedule personal appointments outside of work time. Therefore, you are interested when you hear about a work scheduling practice called "flextime," in which organizations allow people to have some flexibility in regard to when they start and finish their work days. The idea seems promising to you, so you decide to suggest that your immediate supervisor consider adopting some kind of a flextime policy for your organization.

Write an introduction to an informal proposal on the basis of the preceding information.

Exercise 10.2

You are proposing a program that pays employees for suggestions on matters outside of their job responsibilities that result in cost savings to the organization. Employees would be paid a share of the actual savings from suggestions that were implemented. For example, if an administrative assistant made a useful suggestion for reducing the costs of purchasing supplies, that person would be paid 10 percent of the cost savings.

Write a title for this formal proposal and then one or two sentences for each of the other sections listed below.

    a. Title
    b. The problem or opportunity
    c. The purpose of the proposal
    d. One or more alternate solutions
    e. The benefits of the proposed solution(s)
    f. The costs of the proposal

Suggested answers can be found in Appendix C.

11

Grant Proposals

The writing quality of grant proposals frequently makes the difference between getting a grant or not. Still, excellent writing alone is not sufficient for grant proposal success. The other keys to success are as follows: (1) creating individualized proposals, that is, directing your writing to the specific interests of each granting organization; (2) creating well-prepared proposals; and (3) understanding and carefully following all the specific guidelines and criteria each organization requires. Each is discussed in more detail below.

Creating an Individualized Proposal

To create an individualized proposal, you need to learn as much as you can about the granting organization. You can find a great deal of information about an organization by checking its website; attending its events; reading any grant announcements it has issued; and studying proposals it has already approved. You can also attend any grant-writing workshops the organization provides.

Once you have collected such information about the granting organization, you should make a list of the following:

- What terms it uses
- What values it expresses
- What general sensibilities it has
- What goals it has

After you study this list, think of ways you can express a partnership with the funding organization. Write down how your organization can help the funding organization achieve its goals—in other words, *focus on helping instead of needing help.* Think in terms of "we" rather than "you" and "us."

Creating a Well-Prepared Proposal

After you have gathered the above information, you can begin to create your proposal by preparing a rough budget and a framework around which you will develop the details of your program. Start with your budget: it forces you to decide which details to include in the proposal. Be specific about what resources you will need and what their costs will be (including the number of resources required and their estimated prices).

Once you have this rough budget, you should be able to complete the following two sentences. These two sentences can then help guide you through the application process.

Sentence #1

_____ (organization name) requests
_____ ($ total amount) to conduct
_____ (program/project) for
_____ (this/these purposes) to provide
_____ (these benefits) to
_____ (these beneficiaries).

Sentence #2

_____ (organization name) is qualified and
a meritorious choice for such funding because _____

_____
(reasons for qualifications and merits).

Note: The term "qualifications" refers to minimums an organization might specify. The term "merits" refers to any uncommon abilities to carry out a particular grant project.

Following Specific Guidelines

Each funding organization has its own guidelines for writing and submitting grant proposals, and those guidelines *must* be followed in order for your proposal to even be considered. Many organizations post their guidelines on their website. If the guidelines are not posted there, contact the organization to obtain them.

Even though each organization has its own requirements, some commonalities exist with regard to what organizations want in a proposal. Becoming familiar with these common elements can help when you are ready to complete the official proposal. Below we list these elements (in the order in which they usually appear), along with some brief writing pointers.

1. Cover Letter

- Use a personal tone.
- Try to connect personally with the addressee (possibly refer to something shared).

2. Name of the Program or Project (subparts may also be named)

- Create a different name for each grant proposal; be sure the name is short and clear, and avoid cuteness, drama, or humor.
- Use the name in the cover letter and in the proposal title.

3. Summary or Executive Summary

- Write formally.
- Provide more details than you did in the cover letter.
- Provide more description than argumentation.
- Cover the whole range of the proposal.

4. Need or Problem Statement

- Start with more general statements and numbers and then move to specific statements, stories, and individual cases.
- Emphasize persuasive arguments.
- Explain why the need(s) or problem(s) are important.
- Show a gap in existing programs and services.

5. Program or Project Narrative

- Indicate the purpose(s) served (use the terms of the granting organization).
- Describe program activities clearly (use examples and explain as appropriate).
- Indicate why program activities will produce the desired result.
- Show a schedule, especially for multiyear proposals.
- Indicate the personnel positions (by job title [for example, counselor]) and who will undertake which tasks.
- Point out innovations and unique features.

6. Benefits

- Show outcome benefits (end results) and their reasonably predicted levels as much as possible; otherwise, show outputs (activities) and their reasonably predicted levels.
- Indicate the beneficiaries for each benefit.
- Avoid giving trivial or tenuous benefit statements.

7. Qualifications and Merits

- Describe your organization and its history while emphasizing points most relevant to the specific proposal (these descriptions demonstrate sincere interest and commitment).
- Describe your organization's capabilities relative to the pro-

posal, for example, past success, personnel qualifications, facilities required, or other resources (these examples demonstrate performance capability and competence).

• Indicate any factors that make your organization uniquely qualified for the proposed grant, for example, location, access to particular groups, or unique experiences (these factors set your organization apart from other grant-seeking organizations).

• Remember that excellent grant writing is one sign of competence.

8. Budget (and perhaps budget justification)

Grant budgets list the resources to be purchased and their costs (see Figure 11.1, next page). They often also include quantities of items and estimated prices. Budget pointers include the following:

• Write a reasonable budget (not too much or too little relative to proposed activities).

• Include resources your organization and other outside organizations will supply and their sources (for example, another grant, operating budget, or borrowing).

• Be sure estimates are clearly reasonable (price quotes are better than estimates).

• Provide sufficient detail to avoid showing large budget categories with vague descriptions.

• Show budget subdivisions for multiple organizations, organizational units, or years.

• Provide a budget justification that details the content of expenditure categories, explains how specific numbers were calculated, or both; do not, however, provide reasons for funding in a grant budget justification. (Chapter 12 in this book discusses these kinds of budget justifications in greater detail.)

• Write a budget that maximizes expenditures for proposal activities and minimizes overhead expenditures.

Figure 11.1 **Example of Grant Budget**

U.S. DEPARTMENT OF EDUCATION BUDGET INFORMATION NON-CONSTRUCTION PROGRAMS		OMB Control Number: 1894-0008 Expiration Date: 02/28/2011					
Name of Institution/Organization: Patrick Henry School of Science ...		Applicants requesting funding for only one year should complete the column under "Project Year 1." Applicants requesting funding for multi-year grants should complete all applicable columns. Please read all instructions before completing form.					
SECTION A - BUDGET SUMMARY **U.S. DEPARTMENT OF EDUCATION FUNDS**							
Budget Categories	Project Year 1(a)	Project Year 2 (b)	Project Year 3 (c)	Project Year 4 (d)	Project Year 5 (e)	Total (f)	
1. Personnel	$ 20,750	$ 0	$ 0	$ 0	$ 0	$ 20,750	
2. Fringe Benefits	$ 8,100	$ 0	$ 0	$ 0	$ 0	$ 8,100	
3. Travel	$ 900	$ 0	$ 0	$ 0	$ 0	$ 900	
4. Equipment	$ 4,100	$ 27,100	$ 15,900	$ 0	$ 0	$ 47,100	
5. Supplies	$ 7,000	$ 54,750	$ 72,850	$ 0	$ 0	$ 134,600	
6. Contractual	$ 0	$ 0	$ 0	$ 0	$ 0	$ 0	
7. Construction	$ 0	$ 0	$ 0	$ 0	$ 0	$ 0	
8. Other	$ 74,000	$ 97,500	$ 88,850	$ 0	$ 0	$ 260,350	
9. Total Direct Costs (lines 1-8)	$ 114,850	$ 179,350	$ 177,600	$ 0	$ 0	$ 471,800	
10. Indirect Costs*	$ 0	$ 0	$ 0	$ 0	$ 0	$ 0	
11. Training Stipends	$ 0	$ 0	$ 0	$ 0	$ 0	$ 0	
12. Total Costs (lines 9-11)	$ 114,850	$ 179,350	$ 177,600	$ 0	$ 0	$ 471,800	

*Indirect Cost Information *(To Be Completed by Your Business Office)*:

If you are requesting reimbursement for indirect costs on line 10, please answer the following questions:

(1) Do you have an Indirect Cost Rate Agreement approved by the Federal government? [ ] Yes [ ] No
(2) If yes, please provide the following information:
Period Covered by the Indirect Cost Rate Agreement: From: __/__/__ To: __/__/____ (mm/dd/yyyy)
Approving Federal agency: [ ] ED [ ] Other (please specify): _____ The Indirect Cost Rate is _____%
(3) For Restricted Rate Programs (check one) -- Are you using a restricted indirect cost rate that:
[ ] Is included in your approved Indirect Cost Rate Agreement? or, [ ] Complies with 34 CFR 76.564(c)(2)? The Restricted
Indirect Cost Rate is _____%

ED Form No. 524

Source: U.S. Department of Education, Application for Grants Under the Charter Schools Program Non-SEA Planning, Program Design, and Implementation, CFDA #84.282B, p. e11, http://www2.ed.gov/policy/gen/leg/foia/grants/cspatrickhenry schoolofscienceandarts.pdf.

Grant proposals should be reviewed and revised as much as necessary to produce a persuasive piece of writing. In your review, check to be sure that you have followed all criteria listed by the funding organization. Also check to be sure you have expressed yourself appropriately.

Other points are also important to consider in reviewing grant proposals. When writing a grant proposal, you should be sure to do the following:

- Display a positive tone.
- Express points clearly.
- Explain unusual points.
- Choose specific words over general ones and shorter words over longer ones.
- Relate the proposal parts coherently (show that parts relate).
- Create interest (for example, use the active voice).
- Make a compelling case (for example, include vivid stories).
- Unless such words are used by the granting organization, avoid buzzwords, clichés, jargon, and abbreviations (note that some words and phrases fall into more than one category).

Key Points of Chapter 11

- The writing quality of a grant proposal can make the difference between success and failure.
- Make your proposal as individualized as possible, and focus on how you can help the funding organization, not how the organization can help you.
- Start creating your proposal by preparing a rough budget and developing your two-sentence framework.
- Always follow the guidelines the funding organization has specified.
- Double-check to be sure your writing is clear, coherent, and compelling.

EXERCISE FOR CHAPTER 11

Exercise 11.1

You work for the North-South Serving Seniors Organization, which has decided to request funds for assisting low-income senior citizens in their dealings with government agencies. Your supervisor has asked you to complete the parts of the proposal listed below.

Note that for any information that is not specified here, you can imagine the situation, or you can research any number of nonprofit organizations that provide services to senior citizens and use their situations and information for this grant proposal exercise. Also, you can research any number of governments and foundations that fund this kind of project.

a. Complete the following (you know that the title of the program is the Assisting Low-Income Seniors with Government Agencies program, the dollar amount is $250,000 annually, and the time period is five years):

_____ (organization name) requests
_____ ($ total amount) to conduct
_____ (program/project) for
_____ (this/these purposes) to provide
_____ (these benefits) to
_____ (these beneficiaries).

b. Complete the following:

_____ (organization name) is qualified and a meritorious choice for such funding because
_____ (reasons for qualifications and merits).

c. Write a sentence or two on the need(s) or problem(s).
d. Write a sentence or two on the benefits.
e. Write a sentence or two on the expenditures. (Your supervisor has told you that the organization wants money for three government assistance agents, one administrative assistant, program travel, and telephone service. North-South will take care of all other expenses.)

Suggested answers can be found in Appendix C.

12

Budget Justifications

A budget justification is an explanation, in narrative form, of a proposed budget. Note that some people prefer to call this form a "budget narrative" instead of a "budget justification" because the former phrase sounds more neutral, that is, less argumentative and confrontational. Because "budget justification" is still the term most often used, however, we follow that practice here.

Writers of budget justifications might provide up to four kinds of explanations in their justifications. The first two kinds of explanations are commonly seen in budget justifications, and both are generally very specific and matter of fact. The first kind just explains the details, that is, what resources will be purchased. The second kind explains how the numbers in a budget were produced.

The third and fourth kinds of explanations generally provide less specific information; they are often seen as attempts at persuasion. The third kind gives background information on the budget proposal organization or program, including, sometimes, operational details. The fourth kind of explanation provides one or more rationales for funding a proposal. (Note that although some budget proposals include revenues and revenue justifications, in this chapter we focus exclusively on expenditure examples because they are much more common.)

Many organizations use a preset budget proposal format that requires specific information or explanations be provided in or with the budget. No matter what the format is, however, good writing is key to creating an effective budget proposal. In fact, in this time of limited resources and strong competition for funds, producing well-written budget justifications might make the difference between having a higher or lower level of funding approved or even being funded or not.

In the following sections we first describe the general guidelines you should follow to write effective budget justifications. We then address the more specific guidelines you should follow to write the four kinds of explanations listed above.

General Guidelines

Writers of budget justifications should observe the following general guidelines to create effective proposals:

- Above all else, follow the instructions exactly as specified. (Note: If no instructions are provided, follow the conventions used in previous budget proposals.)
- Write from an organizational perspective, not a personal one. For example, avoid the use of "I" and "we."
- Be brief and direct. When possible, start points with *active* verbs and imply the subject (for example, "Proposes adding two consultants. . . ." instead of "The department proposes adding two consultants. . . .").
- Strive for clarity. A funding request is more likely to be rejected if the reader does not readily understand what is being described.
- Be objective. Use an objective tone, not an argumentative one. In other words, describe, do not argue.
- Do not exaggerate or overpromise what the results will be or provide overly optimistic numbers.
- Avoid being overly precise in providing numbers (for example, "493" is easier to consider than "492.87645323" and, in this case, has no practical difference).
- Avoid politically sensitive topics as much as possible.
- Avoid jargon.
- Explain any specialized terminology, including abbreviations.

The following example shows what a proposed budget might look like. Refer to this example when reading the sections that follow.

Example: Proposed Budget

Proposed Budget for Fiscal Year 2015
Gatewick Police Department

Categories	Amounts (in thousands)
Personnel	$715
Supplies	80
Contractual Services	35
Equipment	52
Total	$882

Guidelines for Explaining Details

Expenditure details in budget justifications are meant to help decision makers understand how money is going to be spent and see that the expenditures are reasonable. The details should include answers to the questions of what and how many or how much:

- What will be purchased from the budget?
- How many or how much of different kinds of items will be purchased?

The level of detail can vary in explaining expenditures. In all cases, the level of detail should be enough to allow decision makers to understand the proposed expenditures; however, keep in mind that too much information can be overwhelming. Expenditure explanations should expand on information that is already in the budget, often addressing broad expenditure categories (for example, personnel and supplies). Be sure to use generic and standard terms when writing your expenditure explanations (for example, use personnel titles instead of personal names).

Note that budget decision makers are particularly interested in seeing explanations of new or otherwise changing and larger expenditures and ones that are politically sensitive (for example, additional personnel, travel, and training). For smaller expenditure categories, such as office supplies, a dollar amount is often a sufficient explanation.

The following example shows explanations of details.

Example: Sample Explanations of Details

1. Personnel include twelve sworn law enforcement officers (one chief, two lieutenants, one detective, and eight patrol officers) and two part-time dispatcher-clerks (twenty-five hours a week each).
2. Supplies include fuel, office supplies, and other miscellaneous items.
3. Contractual services include electrical, telephone, and natural gas utilities and training.
4. Equipment includes a new patrol vehicle, a copying machine, and replacements for small pieces of equipment as needed.

Guidelines for Explaining Numbers

Although all numbers in budgets can be explained, the ones of greatest concern to budget decision makers are the expenditure numbers. Budget decision makers are most likely to want to see explanations related to the following:

- Assumptions about and sources of numbers
- Methods of calculation or forecasting
- The relationship between numbers

These budget justifications particularly show information related to prices and quantities. Again, budget decision makers are particularly interested in explanations for new or otherwise changing and larger expenditures and ones that are politically sensitive. They generally look at number explanations both for reasonableness and for places to trim budgets.

The following example shows explanations of numbers.

Example: Sample Explanations of Numbers

1. Personnel estimates were calculated based on the assumption of an anticipated 2 percent raise (or contractually required raise) and an open position rate of 3 percent.
2. Fuel supplies estimate is based on average usage of 20,000 gallons a year at an estimated price of $3.60 per gallon for a bulk contract purchase for a total of $72,000.
3. Contractual services for utilities assume an average increase of prices of 3 percent for the same level of consumption of those services based on estimates of changes in the Consumer Price Index–Urban from the U.S. Bureau of Labor Statistics.
4. Equipment estimates are based on the state contract for police patrol vehicles ($42,000), a price estimate for a midlevel copier from Gatewick Copiers ($4,000), and average experience with replacing small pieces of equipment as necessary (for example, vehicle light bar, radio, and computer equipment).

Guidelines for Explaining Background Information

Writers of budget justifications include background information to provide context or details about the organization or program represented by a budget proposal. Budget decision makers might specify the background information they want; we recommend against inserting any background information that is not requested.

Background information may include historical accounts or information; operational details or plans; or descriptions of such features as mission statements, activities, responsibilities, legal authority, functions, services, or service provision sites. You should provide these kinds of explanations in an objective and descriptive rather than an argumentative fashion. Be sure they are brief and consistent with past versions of the same budget justification.

Note: In some cases, background information may be provided on request or in other forums or documents.

The following example shows explanations of background information.

> **Example: Sample Explanations of Background Information**
>
> 1. The central purpose of the Gatewick Police Department is to protect the lives, property, and rights of all the people in the city and to maintain order while enforcing the laws fairly and impartially.
> 2. One or two police officers are on patrol at all times, and one or two others are ready to respond at all times.
> 3. The average emergency response time for a sworn officer of the Gatewick Police Department to arrive at the scene of an emergency is three minutes.
> 4. The Gatewick Police Department investigates 1,400 reported crimes a year (based on a three-year average).

Guidelines for Explaining Rationales

Budget rationales explain why funding a budget proposal is a good idea. (Some background information also serves this purpose.) Budget decision makers often do not want rationales of any kind, but when they do, they generally specify what they want in written or oral instructions.

Budget rationales generally say that good things will occur and bad things will be avoided if the proposed budget is approved. Some of the more common rationales are descriptions of the services that will be provided; the positive goals that will be pursued and attained; the benefits that will be created; and the costs that will be avoided.

As with budget proposal backgrounds, these kinds of explanations should be stated objectively and descriptively rather than in an argumentative fashion. They should be brief and consistent with past versions of the same budget justification. Similar to budget proposal background information, budget rationales also may be provided on request or in other forums or documents. The following example shows explanations of rationales.

Example: Sample Explanations of Rationales

1. The Gatewick Police Department solves 60 percent of reported crimes.
2. The Gatewick Police Department maintains traffic safety.
3. The Gatewick Police Department provides quality police service in partnership with the community and strives to attain the highest degree of ethical behavior and professional conduct at all times.
4. The additional resources in the proposed Safe Streets Program Grant to the state for a Breathalyzer and a radar gun (only $1,000 for the City of Gatewick) will reduce traffic accidents by 10 percent and result in one fewer fatality, five fewer severe injuries, and a $200,000 reduction in property damage each year.

Key Points of Chapter 12

- A budget justification is an explanation, in narrative form, of a proposed budget.
- Writers of budget justifications might write up to four kinds of explanations: explanations of details, explanations of numbers, explanations of background information, and explanations of rationales.
- Writers must follow all specified guidelines in creating the budget proposal.
- Writing should be brief, direct, clear, and objective.

EXERCISE FOR CHAPTER 12

Exercise 12.1

The director of the Wickgate Public Library has asked you to write specific kinds of budget justifications for the Proposed Budget for the Wickgate Public Library.

a. The Wickgate Public Library Proposed Budget shows a total for personnel salaries of $475,000. Information about these salaries appears in the table below.

Personnel Table

Title	Number	Annual Salary
Director	1	$65,000
Librarians	7 @ $50,000 each	$350,000
Administrative Staff	1	$35,000
Custodial Staff	1	$25,000
Total	10	$475,000

Write a one-sentence budget justification "explaining details" for personnel salaries. All the information you need appears in the personnel table. You do not have to do any calculations.

b. The Wickgate Public Library Proposed Budget shows a total for employer taxes of $60,087.50. Information about employer taxes includes the facts that the total for personnel salaries is $475,000 and that employer taxes are expressed as a percentage of personnel salaries. Information on specific employer taxes follows in the Employer Taxes Table, which shows the total rate for employer taxes and the employer taxes calculation.

Employer Taxes Table

Tax	Rate (%)
FICA (Social Security and Medicare)	7.65
State and Federal Unemployment Taxes	3.00
Workers' Compensation	2.00
Total	12.65

On the basis of the total tax rate in this table, the Employer Taxes Calculation is $475,000 × 0.1265 = $60,087.50.

In a sentence or two, write a budget justification "explaining numbers" for employer taxes. All the information you need appears above. You do not have to do any calculations.

c. The Wickgate Public Library director wants to use the proposed budget in discussions with representatives of other organizations about grants and asks you to write a budget justification explaining background information. In your preparatory research, you find the following information in the latest annual report:

- The Wickgate Public Library's motto is "The mindful life of the mind."
- The Wickgate Public Library provides information to patrons on-site and through its website, has related programming, and is a welcoming public place for individuals and groups.
- Hours of operation are 9:00 a.m. to 6:00 p.m. daily, Monday through Saturday.
- The director and the seven librarians acquire and manage material, staff the circulation and reference desks, assist patrons, and organize and lead some programs.

In a few sentences, write a budget justification "explaining background information."

d. The Wickgate Public Library director wants to use the proposed budget in discussions with representatives of other organizations about grants and asks you to write a budget justification explaining rationales. In your research, you find the following information in the latest annual report representing averages over the last few years:

- Wickgate population: 23,000
- Materials circulated: 126,000 (print, other physical media, and electronic media items)
- Visits to the library: 13,000 (physical and virtual)
- Circulating items acquired: 7,000

- On-site programs: 80 (for example, "Story Time" and "Photography for Fun" programs)
- On-site meetings: 65
- Reference questions answered: 4,200

In a few sentences, write a budget justification "explaining rationales."

Suggested answers can be found in Appendix C.

13

Rules

The skills needed to write effective rules are similar to those needed to write the other public sector documents we discuss in this book, but some differences also exist. In addition, the whole concept of rule writing differs from some of the more familiar projects we see in the public sector. In this chapter we first explain what a rule is and what kinds of rules exist. We then describe how to write them effectively.

Rules: An Overview

Broadly speaking, rules guide behavior by indicating appropriate and inappropriate behavior in various situations. Written rules can express three different kinds of behavior: you *must* do X, you *must not* do X, or you *may* do X.

In the public sector, rules are either binding or nonbinding. Binding rules have the force of law and create legal rights and responsibilities. Binding rules include laws, administrative rules, and contracts. In contrast, nonbinding rules are not legally enforceable; they are advisory or interpretive statements that can be changed at the discretion of the rule-writing entity. Nonbinding rules include an organization's or its representatives' statements about future plans or policy interpretations and advice of any kind. Examples include such statements as "We plan on doing X" (plan), "We interpret the law in this way" (interpretation), and "Do not drive into standing water deeper than a few inches" (advice). Much of the time, but not always, instructions on how to proceed, such as in an application process or a procedures manual, are nonbinding.

Note: Binding rules are usually more difficult to write because writers first need to become familiar with each rule's legal authority and be sure they correctly interpret the authority and do not exceed or contradict the authority. They also need to become familiar with the appropriate general legal requirements, which might indicate mandatory and prohibited terms, formats, and wording. Writers should check with appropriate legal professionals for more information on binding rules.

Guidelines for Writing Rules

As might be expected, numerous guidelines exist for writing rules. Here, because of space limitations, we provide an overview of what is entailed in rule writing. You will be able to write effective rules after reading these guidelines, but you might want to check the resources listed in the back of this book, in libraries, and online for more information on particular aspects of rule writing.

Your rules will be more effective if you adopt the following formal process: prepare; organize; write; and review, revise, and proofread. Each step is discussed in turn below.

Step 1: Prepare

The process of preparing helps the writer become familiar with the content needed to write rules. Content can be determined by looking at the following concepts found in all rules:

- *Purpose:* Purposes are the goals or end conditions that rules are designed to achieve. They are usually stated in a simple way, for example, "The purpose [of this rule] is to protect public health and safety."
- *Audiences:* Audiences are the people who have reasons to read the rules. Audiences might include external groups (for example, the public) and internal groups (for example, the people who administer or enforce the rules).

- *Applicability:* Applicability refers to the conditions in which the rules apply. People will read rules to see whether the rules apply to their specific situations.
- *Subject matter:* Subject matter refers to what the rules are about; the title of the rule usually reflects the subject matter.
- *Processes:* Processes refer to the series of events involved in rules. For example, in an application process, someone prepares and submits an application, and someone else handles the application.
- *Questions:* Questions anticipate what readers might ask. Writers should keep in mind that people consult rules to answer their questions, which are often very specific. Therefore, writers often develop a series of frequently asked questions, based on the writer's experience regarding what questions are usually asked about rules. Most questions deal with costs and benefits and/or the basic questions of who, what, when, why, where, and how.

Note: In addition to determining what content needs to be covered in each rule, writers should also prepare by reviewing previously written rules on the same subject (if available). Even poorly written rules provide relevant information, terms, and questions.

Step 2: Organize

After completing the preparation process, writers next need to organize the information they have gathered. The most important questions when organizing are as follows: What groups of information belong together, and in what sequence should information be given to make the most sense to the reader?

The multiple relationships among the different kinds of information in rules make organizing them difficult. Therefore, we recommend that you first develop an outline or a series of outlines to figure out the best way to organize the information. You can develop your outline as follows:

- Decide on a title for your rules. The title should be succinct but should provide enough information for the reader to understand what the rules are about.
- Put the most important information first, and place general information before specific information.
- Place information in a logical order (for example, chronological).
- Use headings and subheadings to help you place your information in a logical order.

Below is an example of an outline created on the topic of plumbing rules. The first part of the outline places in a logical order the information property owners and their agents might seek when they need to deal with plumbing work in their community. The second part of the outline places in a logical order the information a plumber might need to know before starting a plumbing job in the same community.

Example: Plumbing Rules Outline

   I. Rules for Those Responsible for Plumbing Work
      (Property Owners and Their Agents)
     A. Purposes of Rules
     B. Definitions
       1. Plumbing Work
       2. Those Responsible for Plumbing Work
       3. Licensed Plumber
     C. Responsibilities
       1. Duty to Have Plumbing Work Done by Licensed
         Plumber
       2. Duty to Obtain a Permit before Certain Plumbing
         Work Is Done
       3. Duty to Have Certain Plumbing Work Inspected
     D. Penalties
  II. Rules for Plumbers
     A. Purposes of Rules
     B. Definitions

```
    1. Plumbing Work
    2. Licensed Plumber
  C. Responsibilities
    1. Duty to Follow Plumbing Rules
    2. Duty to Obtain a Permit before Certain Plumbing
       Work Is Done
    3. Duty to Have Certain Plumbing Work Inspected
  D. Obtaining a Plumbing License
  E. Substantive Plumbing Rules
    1. Generic Plumbing Code Adopted
    2. Local Exceptions
  F. Penalties
```

Step 3: Write

After you finish organizing, you will be ready to write. As you will see, the process of writing rules differs in some respects from other types of writing in the public sector. For example, when you write a rule, you are not only informing people of something, you are also directly affecting their future actions. In other words, writing rules requires choosing the correct words and placing them in the correct order so people know clearly what they must, must not, or may do. Your words directly affect their subsequent behavior.

In this section we focus on the three main components of writing rules: words, sentences, and headings.

Words

As with any writing, rules are more easily understood when the wording is clear and concise. (Review especially Chapters 2 and 3 in this book for more on this subject.) In addition, to ensure that your words lead to certain actions from the readers, you also need to focus on the following:

• Use concrete words instead of abstract ones.

- Use a few inclusive, general words instead of many overly specific ones. For example, in the following rule, the words "harm" and "plant" could easily replace many of the more specific ones used:

  50.10 Trees, shrubs, plants, grass, and other vegetation

  (a) General injury. No person shall prune, cut, carry away, pull up, dig, fell, destroy, set fire to, burn, scorch, carve, paint, mark, or in any manner interfere with, tamper, mutilate, misuse, disturb, or damage any tree, shrub, plant, grass, flower, or part thereof. . . .

- Use the same words consistently throughout rules. Readers can easily become confused by changes in terms because they do not know whether or how a new word or term differs from the one previously used in the rules.
- Place negative words (for example, "no" and "not") early in the sentences so the reader knows immediately that something is being prohibited or excluded.
- Place the subjects early in the sentences so the reader knows immediately who is acting or what is being explained.
- Use active verbs when possible and place them early in the sentences.
- Place phrases and lists in the latter half of the sentences.

Sentences

Rules writers must also focus on the kinds of sentences they write and their placement in the rule. Sentences in rules tend to be of two types:

- *Action sentences:* Action sentences indicate what someone must, must not, or may do. People read rules for action sentences, so these sentences should always be written first in a paragraph.
- *Explanation sentences:* Explanation sentences elaborate on the meaning of action sentences and provide the necessary details.

Other guidelines for effective rules sentences are as follows:

- General sentences should usually precede more specific ones. General sentences help clarify the context in which specific sentences can be better understood.
- One-sentence paragraphs are preferable to longer paragraphs. When two or more sentences are necessary, be sure to make the first sentence the topic sentence.
- Exceptions to rules should usually be given in their own sentences, with general points made before more specific ones.

  Note: In some cases, however, a sentence stating an exception will be more clear and concise when the specific point is given first. For example, the rule "No animals allowed, except service animals" would read better if it was revised to read "Only service animals are allowed."
- Exceptions to exceptions can confuse the reader, so, when possible, try to write sentences in inclusive rather than exclusive terms (that is, add categories together rather than subtract something from a category). For example, a confusing recycling rule might read as follows:

  All trash goes into the garbage bin, except for recyclable material, which goes into the recycling bin, except for soiled recycling materials, which go into the garbage bin.

  Notice here that trash is divided by exclusion into two parts (recyclable materials and everything else), and then recyclable materials are divided by exclusion into two parts (recyclable materials are clean or soiled). The following sentences cover the same situation but *include* soiled recyclable materials with garbage rather than *exclude* them from the recycling bin:

  All trash goes into the recycling bin or the garbage bin. Clean recyclable material goes into the recycling bin; all other materials, including soiled recyclable material, go into the garbage bin.
- Sentences should be short and clear. Rules need to be focused, direct, and, at times, even blunt to both attract and keep the reader's attention. For example:

Wordy: Please respect the environment and do not harm plants or animals.

Better: Do not harm plants or animals.

Headings

Take special care regarding how you word headings because people read headings first to find the information they seek. Headings should have the following characteristics:

- Headings should be short and consistent with the words in the rest of the text.
- Headings should contain words that readers are seeking.
- When possible, headings should be written in the following order: verb or other action words (that is, words that convey an action of some kind) first, followed by nouns, followed by any adjectives necessary to qualify the nouns.

Below is an example of how you can turn an outline (in this case, the outline shown earlier in this chapter) into effective headings. As you can see, the information in the revised headings is clearer, more direct, and generally shorter than the information in the original outline (the strikethrough text indicates deletions; the italicized text indicates new wording).

Example: Headings for Plumbing Rules

   I. ~~Rules Those~~ *Requirements for Persons* Responsible for Plumbing Work (Property Owners and Their Agents)
     A. Purposes ~~of Rules~~
     B. ~~Definitions~~ *Terms Defined*
       1. Plumbing Work
       2. ~~Those~~ *Persons* Responsible for Plumbing Work
       3. Licensed Plumber

C. Responsibilities
   1. ~~Duty to Have Plumbing Work Done by~~ Licensed Plumber
   2. ~~Duty to Obtain a Permit before Certain Plumbing Work Is Done~~ *Permits*
   3. ~~Duty to Have Certain Plumbing Work Inspected~~ *Inspections*
D. Penalties

II. ~~Rules~~ *Requirements* for Plumbers
  A. Purposes ~~of Rules~~
  B. ~~Definitions~~ *Terms Defined*
   1. Plumbing Work
   2. Licensed Plumber
  C. Responsibilities
   1. ~~Duty to Follow~~ Plumbing Rules
   2. ~~Duty to Obtain a Permit before Certain Plumbing Work Is Done~~ *Plumbing Permits*
   3. ~~Duty to Have Certain Plumbing Work Inspected~~ *Plumbing Inspections*
  D. ~~Obtaining a~~ Plumbing License
  E. ~~Substantive Plumbing~~ *Specific* Rules
   1. ~~Generic Plumbing~~ Code Adopted
   2. ~~Local~~ Exceptions
  F. Penalties

Step 4: Review, Revise, and Proofread

The process of reviewing, revising, and proofreading occurs in three stages. First, you should review, revise, and proofread rules as you would any other form of writing (see Chapters 2, 3, and 4 in this book for more on these processes).

Second, once you have completed any changes you wish to make, give the rules to experts in the subject matter you are addressing (give the rules to legal experts, too, if the rules are binding) and ask for their feedback. Once you receive their feedback, you might then need to revise and proofread again.

Finally, we recommend that an official or officials review the rules after they have been in effect for a short period of time. That review should look at both the questions that readers ask about the rules and the effects of the rules. After that review, some revisions might need to be made to create a more effective set of rules.

Key Points of Chapter 13

- Written rules express three different kinds of behavior: you *must* do X, you *must not* do X, or you *may* do X.
- You can write more effective rules by adopting the following process: preparing; organizing; writing; and reviewing, revising, and proofreading.
- Preparing involves becoming familiar with the content that needs to be covered in each rule.
- Organizing involves determining what information should be grouped together in the rules and in what sequence that information should be given.
- Writing rules involves not only writing clearly and concisely but also providing the correct words and placing them in the correct order so people know what they must, must not, or may do.
- The step of reviewing, revising, and proofreading rules should also include a review by experts in the subject matter both before and after the rules go into effect.

EXERCISE FOR CHAPTER 13

Exercise 13.1

Your supervisor has assigned you to write a new set of more effective rules restricting behavior on city property. Write the new rules on the basis of the information in the old rules (see next page) and the guidelines in this chapter. (If writing all of them seems too challenging, you can write one or a few of them.)

City of Eastwest
Rules about Behavior on City Property

Preservation of property. Creating any hazard to persons or
things, climbing upon the roof or any part of a building, or
willfully destroying, damaging, or removing any property or any
part thereof, is prohibited.

Conformity with signs and directions. All persons in and on
city property shall comply with official signs of a prohibitory
or directory nature, and with the directions of security force
personnel or other authorized individuals.

Gambling. Participating in games for money or other personal
property, the operation of gambling devices, the conduct of a
lottery or pool, or the selling or purchasing of lottery tickets, is
prohibited on city premises.

Disturbances. Disorderly conduct, or conduct which creates
loud and unusual noise, or which impedes ingress to or egress
from public property or facilities, or otherwise obstructs the
usual use of entrances, foyers, corridors, offices, elevators,
stairways, and parking lots, or which otherwise tends to
impede or disturb the public employees in the performance
of their duties, or which otherwise impedes or disturbs the
general public in transacting business or obtaining the services
provided on property, is prohibited.

Suggested answers can be found in Appendix C.

Appendix A

Troublesome Words and Phrases

Table A.1

Common Homonyms That Can Be Confused

aid	to help
aide	a person who assists
altar	a church table
alter	to change something
arc	a part of a circle
ark	a ship or other vessel
ascent	a climb
assent	an act of agreeing; to agree
bite	to use one's teeth to cut into something
byte	a group of binary digits (usually eight)
bloc	an alliance
block	a solid item; to restrict passage
cannon	a large gun
canon	a body of law
capital	the seat of government
capitol	the building where legislative body meets
complement	to bring to completion
compliment	to praise

council	an advisory body
counsel	a lawyer; advice
discreet	careful; confidential
discrete	individually separate
elicit	to draw out
illicit	unlawful
forego	to precede
forgo	to refrain from
foreword	an introduction to a book
forward	toward the front
forth	forward
fourth	following the third
incite	to provoke
insight	a deep understanding
it's	contraction of "it is"
its	belonging to a thing
lead	metal
led	showed the way
meet	to connect with
mete	to dispense justice
precedence	priority in importance
precedents	earlier courses of actions now considered guides
principal	the head of a school; the amount of a loan
principle	a legal, moral, or scientific rule
resister	a person or thing that fights against an action or effect
resistor	a device designed to control electrical current
right	correct; opposite of left
rite	a ritual

rout	to force out
route	a path of travel
stationary	not moving
stationery	a piece of writing paper
straight	not crooked
strait	a narrow passage of water
their	belonging to other people or things
there	a place
they're	contraction of "they are"
threw	to propel with force
through	to move in one side and out the other
to	toward
too	also
two	a couple
tort	a wrongful act leading to liability
torte	a dessert
verses	a group of lines in poem or song
versus	as opposed to
who's	contraction of "who is"
whose	belonging to a person
you're	contraction of "you are"
your	belonging to you

Table A.2

Commonly Misspelled Words

absence	knowledge
accessible	manageable
accidentally	marshal
accommodate	mischievous
achieve	misspelled
acknowledgment	necessary
apparent	numerous
arctic	occasion
ascend	occur
athlete	occurrence
athletics	parallel
attendance	parliament
believe	pastime
beneficial	permissible
benefited	perseverance
calendar	possession
cemetery	precede
chief	preference
commitment	preferred
committed	prejudice
conceive	prevalent
conscience	privilege
convenient	proceed
curiosity	questionnaire
curriculum	referred
definitely	reminisce
descendant	rhyme
desirable	rhythm
desperate	sacrifice
dissatisfied	secretary
embarrass	separate
exaggerate	similar
existence	sophomore
familiar	subtly
forty	thorough
gauge	tomorrow
grammar	tragedy
guidance	transferred
harass	unanimous
humorous	unconscious
independence	unnecessary
irrelevant	vacuum
irresistible	weird
judgment	wholly

Table A.3

Long Phrases That Can Be Shortened

Instead of	Use
as a matter of fact	in fact
at a later date	later
at all times	always
at the present time	now
at this point in time	now
at this time	now
because of the fact that	because
become cognizant of	learn
despite the fact that	despite, although
due to the fact that	because
during the time that	during, while
enclosed please find	enclosed is
few in number	few
for the purpose of	to
for the reason that	because
in compliance with your request	as you requested
in many cases	often, frequently
in order to	to
in spite of	despite
in spite of the fact that	despite, although
in the event that	if
in the near future	soon (or specify date)
in view of the fact that	because, in view of
inasmuch as	because
large number of	many
please be advised that	please note
prior to	before
subsequent to	after
the majority of	most
this writer	I, me
until such time	when, until

Table A.4

Words That Can Be Confused

adverse; averse	"Adverse" refers to something harmful or unfavorable and usually refers to things ("We had adverse weather conditions."); "averse" means a strong feeling of dislike ("She was averse to eating peanut butter.").
affect; effect	"Affect" is usually used as a verb and means to have an impact on or influence on; "effect" is usually used as a noun and means a result or consequence of something.
altar; alter	An "altar" (noun) is a table used in church; to "alter" (verb) is to change something.
amount; number	Use "amount" when referring to a mass or bulk ("Sam approached the new job with a growing amount of confidence."); use "number" for countable things ("We had a number of items to cover on the agenda.")
appraise; apprise	To "appraise" is to put a value on something; to "apprise" is to inform.
between; among	"Between" is usually used to indicate a relationship between two things; "among" is used to indicate relationships among more than two things.
can; may	"Can" usually refers to the ability to do something; "may" refers to the possibility of doing something.
capital; capitol	A "capital" is a seat of government (it can also mean a form of wealth); a "capitol" is a building in which a legislative body meets.
complement; compliment	To "complement" is to complete something; to "compliment" is to praise.
connote; denote	To "connote" is to imply or convey an additional idea; to "denote" is to indicate the literal meaning.
continual; continuous	"Continual" means something is intermittent or frequently repeated; "continuous" means something that never stops.
criteria; criterion	A "criterion" is a standard by which to measure something; "criteria" is the plural of the word.
currently; presently	"Currently" means right now; "presently" means soon.

desert; dessert	A "desert" is a dry, arid place; a "dessert" is a sweet treat at the end of a meal.
different from; different than	Generally, use "different from."
disinterested; uninterested	To be "disinterested" is to be neutral with regard to the outcome of something (a judge should be disinterested); to be "uninterested" is to be unconcerned.
economic; economical	"Economic" means related to finance; "economical" means being thrifty.
emigrate; immigrate	"Emigrate" is to leave a place; "immigrate" is to go to a place. A person emigrates *from* a country; a person immigrates *to* a country.
eminent; imminent	"Eminent" means well known; "imminent" means something is about to happen.
ensure; insure	To "ensure" is to guarantee that something will or will not happen; to "insure" is to guard against financial loss. Thus, you might ensure that your meeting time is correct by calling ahead and confirming the time; you would insure your car to cover any loss in case of an accident on your way to the meeting.
every day; everyday	"Every day" is an adverbial phase (think "each day"); "everyday" is an adjective meaning average. ("Every day some people live everyday lives.")
explicit; implicit	If something is "explicit," it is stated clearly; if it is "implicit," it is implied.
farther; further	"Farther" is used for physical distance ("The house is seven miles farther down the road."); "further" is used for figurative distance ("That could not be further from the truth.").
fewer; less	Use "fewer" for things you can count ("Fewer people came to the meeting."); use "less" for mass amounts ("We have less coffee than I expected.").
flammable; inflammable	These words mean the same thing. "Flammable" has become the preferred term because too many people mistakenly think that "inflammable" means "not flammable."
fortuitous; fortunate	"Fortuitous" means something happens by chance (whether the result is good or bad); "fortunate" means something occurs by good luck.
hangar; hanger	A "hangar" is the place where airplanes are kept; use "hanger" for everything else.

lay; lie	The word "lay" always has a direct object ("Please lay the books on the table."); "lie" does not have a direct object, that is, it does not transfer action to an object ("The ship lies on the bottom of the ocean.").
literally; figuratively	Use "literally" to mean actually; use "figuratively" to mean not actually.
militate; mitigate	"Militate" means to have a major effect on (and usually takes the preposition "against": "These differences will militate against coming to an agreement."). "Mitigate" means to soften or make less severe ("These mitigating circumstances will help in her hearing.").
ordinance; ordnance	An "ordinance" is a piece of legislation enacted by a municipality; "ordnance" is military artillery.
people; persons	Use "people" for large groups; use "persons" for small groups.
principal; principle	As you probably learned in school, "principal" is used to refer to a person ("The principal is my pal."), but "principal" also has two other meanings: as a noun it means the amount of a loan that needs to be repaid, and as an adjective it means primary ("Better service was their principal objective."). A "principle" is a legal, moral, or scientific rule or foundational belief ("Better service was their guiding principle.").
proved; proven	Generally, use "proved" as the verb; use "proven" as an adjective.
stationary; stationery	"Stationary" means unchanging or staying in one place; "stationery" is writing paper.
that; which	"That" is used to introduce a restrictive word or phrase, that is, a word or phrase needed to have the sentence make sense. "Which" is used to introduce a nonrestrictive word or phrase, that is, a word or phrase that just provides information not essential to the meaning of the sentence. See Chapter 2 for more on this distinction.
toward; towards	"Toward" is the preferred usage in the United States.
use; utilize	Generally, the word "use" is preferred.

Table A.5

Potentially Biased Terms and Suggested Replacements

Instead of	*Use*
chairman	chair, presiding officer
confined to a wheelchair	uses a wheelchair
congressman	congressional representative
fireman	firefighter
forefather	ancestor
foreman	supervisor
handicapped	person with a disability
housewife	homemaker
Indian	Native American
mailman	mail carrier, postal worker
mankind	humanity, human beings
manmade	manufactured, fabricated
manpower	personnel, staff, workforce
newsman	journalist, reporter
Oriental	Asian
policeman	police officer
salesman	salesperson, sales representative
spokesman	representative, spokesperson
statesman	leader
watchman	guard
weatherman	weather forecaster, meteorologist
workman	worker, laborer
workmanlike	skillful

Appendix B

Documentation Styles

Perhaps the best way to think about documentation is to realize that its purpose is twofold. First, you provide documentation to give credit to others for their words and for their ideas that are not common knowledge. Second, you provide documentation to give readers enough information to locate any source easily. Generally, that information includes, in some format, the name of the author(s) you are citing, the name of the work being cited, and the publication data (place of publication, name of publisher, year of publication) for the work being cited. With that information, readers can go to a library or online and find the source.

Conventions used to cite sources vary, but, as we mentioned in Chapter 9, two styles are commonly used in the public sector. One is the notes (footnotes or endnotes) documentation style, with a bibliography at the end of the document. The other is the in-text citations documentation style, with a reference list at the end of the document. The notes/bibliography style is one of the systems of documentation shown in the *Chicago Manual of Style* (sixteenth edition); the in-text citation/reference list style is the system of documentation shown in the *Publication Manual of the American Psychological Association* (sixth edition).

Here we present some of the more common types of citations in each of these styles (where possible, we show the same sources so similarities and differences can be easily seen). Consult the manuals for more examples.

Notes/Bibliography Documentation Style
(Chicago Style)

Note: N indicates note citation; B indicates bibliographical entry.

Books

Note: The general format for books is as follows: full name of author(s) or editor(s), title of book, place of publication, name of publisher, year of publication, and (for notes only) the page number(s) of the quotation or point being referenced.

Books with Single Author or Editor

N: 1. Bryan A. Garner, *HBR Guide to Better Business Writing* (Boston: Harvard Business Review Press, 2012), 23.

B: Garner, Bryan A. *HBR Guide to Better Business Writing.* Boston: Harvard Business Review Press, 2012.

Note: When the city of publication is not well known, add the two-letter postal code of the state after the name of the city (see next example). Exception: When the place of publication is Washington, DC, include "DC" to make it clear that you are referring to the U.S. capital rather than the state.

N: 2. Timothy Burns, ed., *Recovering Reason: Essays in Honor of Thomas L. Pangle* (Lanham, MD: Lexington Books, 2010), 19.

B: Burns, Timothy, ed. *Recovering Reason: Essays in Honor of Thomas L. Pangle.* Lanham, MD: Lexington Books, 2010.

Books with Two or Three Authors

N: 1. Libby Allison and Miriam F. Williams, *Writing for the Government* (New York: Pearson/Longman, 2008), 27.

B: Allison, Libby, and Mariam F. Williams. *Writing for the Government*. New York: Pearson/Longman, 2008.

Books with More Than Three Authors

N: 1. Vernon L. Quinsey et al., *Violent Offenders: Appraising and Managing Risk*, 2nd ed. (New York: American Psychological Association, 2005), 19.

B: Quinsey, Vernon L., Grant T. Harris, Marnie E. Rice, and Catherine A. Cormier. *Violent Offenders: Appraising and Managing Risk*. 2nd ed. New York: American Psychological Association, 2005.

Books with an Organization as Author

N: 1. University of Chicago Press, *The Chicago Manual of Style*, 16th ed. (Chicago: University of Chicago Press, 2010), 655.

B: University of Chicago Press. *The Chicago Manual of Style*. 16th ed. Chicago: University of Chicago Press, 2010.

Chapter in a Multi-Authored Book

Note: In this type of citation, the chapter title is provided before the book title, and the inclusive pages of the chapter are given in the bibliographical entry.

N: 1. James M. Banovetz, "The Challenges of Community Government," in *Managing Small Cities and Counties: A Practical Guide*, ed. James M. Banovetz, Drew A. Dolan, and John W. Swain (Washington, DC: International City/County Management Association, 1994), 10.

B: Banovetz, James M. "The Challenges of Community Government." In *Managing Small Cities and Counties: A Practical Guide*, edited by James M. Banovetz, Drew A. Dolan, and John W. Swain, 3–27. Washington, DC: International City/County Management Association, 1994.

Journal Articles

Notes: (1) The general format for journal articles is as follows: full name of author(s); title of article; title of journal; volume number of journal; issue number of journal (if available); season or month (if the journal is usually cited this way); year of issue; and page number(s) (in note, the page number of the quotation; in bibliography, the inclusive pages of the article). (2) Many writers are now consulting articles online. If you do so, we recommend that you add, at the end of the citation, either the Digital Object Identifier (DOI) (a unique number assigned to the article to make it easier to locate) or the uniform resource locator (URL) (a specific address on the Internet). The DOI tends to be a more reliable identifier. Several examples are shown below.

Journal Article with Single Author

N: 1. Irene Rubin, "The Great Unraveling: Federal Budgeting, 1998–2006," *Public Administration Review* 67, no. 4 (2007): 609.

B: Rubin, Irene. "The Great Unraveling: Federal Budgeting, 1998–2006." *Public Administration Review* 67, no. 4 (2007): 608–17.

Journal Article with Two Authors

N: 1. Donald F. Norris and Christopher G. Reddick, "Local E-Government in the United States: Transformation or Incremental Change?" *Public Administration Review* 72, no. 1 (2013): 173, doi:10.1111/j.1540-6210. 2012.02647.x.

B: Norris, Donald F., and Christopher G. Reddick. "Local E-Government in the United States: Transformation or Incremental Change?" *Public Administration Review* 72, no. 1 (2013): 165–75. doi:10.1111/j.1540-6210.2012.02647.x.

Journal Article with Three Authors

N: 1. Roberto Cabaleiro, Enrique Buch, and Antonio Vaamonde, "Developing a Method to Assessing the Municipal Financial Health," *American Review of Public Administration* 43, no. 6 (2013): 749, doi:10.1177/0275074012451523.

B: Cabaleiro, Roberto, Enrique Buch, and Antonio Vaamonde. "Developing a Method to Assessing the Municipal Financial Health." *American Review of Public Administration* 43, no. 6 (2013): 729–51. doi:10.1177/0275074012451523.

Journal Article with More Than Three Authors

N: 1. Marc Esteve et al., "Organizational Collaboration in the Public Sector: Do Chief Executives Make a Difference?" *Journal of Public Administration Research and Theory* 23, no. 4 (2013): 936, doi:10.1093/jopart/mus035.

B: Esteve, Marc, George Boyne, Vincenta Sierra, and Tamyko Ysa. "Organizational Collaboration in the Public Sector: Do Chief Executives Make a Difference?" *Journal of Public Administration Research and Theory* 23, no. 4 (2013): 927–52. doi:10.1093/jopart/mus035.

Other Common Citations

Magazine Article

N: 1. Marina Krakovsky, "The Words That Bind," *Discover*, November 2013, 29.

B: Krakovsky, Marina. "The Words That Bind." *Discover*, November 2013, 28–30.

Newspaper Article

N: 1. Bill Ruthhart, "Speed Cameras' Potential Windfall," *Chicago Tribune*, October 12, 2013, 1.

B: Ruthhart, Bill. "Speed Cameras' Potential Windfall." *Chicago Tribune*, October 12, 2013, 1, 4.

Government Document

N: 1. U.S. Census Bureau, *Statistical Abstract of the United States* (Washington, DC: U.S. Government Printing Office, 2000).

B: U.S. Census Bureau. *Statistical Abstract of the United States*. Washington, DC: U.S. Government Printing Office, 2000.

Website

N: 1. Jessica Clements et al., "General Format," Purdue Online Writing Lab, last modified October 12, 2011, http://owl.english.purdue.edu/owl/resource/717/13/.

B: Clements, Jessica, Elizabeth Angeli, Karen Schiller, S. C. Gooch, Laurie Pinkert, and Allen Brizee. "General Format." Purdue Online Writing Lab. Last modified October 12, 2011. http://owl.english. purdue.edu/owl/resource/717/13/.

Note: If you cannot determine the publication date or the date of the last modification, insert instead the date you accessed the site.

Blog Entry

N: 1. Gary Becker, "Ceilings on Government Debt, Taxes, and Government Spending," *Becker-Posner Blog* (blog), October 6, 2013, http://www.becker-posner-blog.com/2013/10/ceilings-on-government-debt-taxes-and-government-spending-becker.html.

B: Becker, Gary. "Ceilings on Government Debt, Taxes, and Government Spending." *Becker-Posner Blog* (blog). http://www.becker-posner-blog.com/2013/10/ceilings-on-government-debt-taxes-and-government-spending-becker.html.

In-Text Citation/Reference Style (APA Style)

Note: IT indicates in-text citation; *R* indicates reference entry.

Books

Note: The general format for books is as follows: (1) in the in-text citation, provide the last name(s) of author(s) or editor(s), year of publication, and page number of the quotation or point being referenced; (2) in the reference citation, provide last name(s) and first initial(s) of author(s) or editor(s), year of publication, title of book, place of publication, and name of publisher.

Books with Single Author or Editor

IT: (Garner, 2012, p. 23) [or, if the author's name appears in the text, "Garner (2012, p. 23) states . . ."].

R: Garner, B. A. (2012). *HBR guide to better business writing.* Boston, MA: Harvard Business Review Press.

IT: (Burns, 2010, p. 19) [or "Burns (2010, p. 19) states . . ."].

R: Burns, T. (Ed.) (2010). *Recovering reason: Essays in honor of Thomas L. Pangle.* Lanham, MD: Lexington Books.

Books with Two Authors

IT: (Allison & Williams, 2008, p. 27) [or "Allison and Williams (2008, p. 27) state . . ."].

R: Allison, L., & Williams, M. F. (2008). *Writing for the government.* New York, NY: Pearson/Longman.

Books with Three to Five Authors

IT: (Quinsey, Harris, Rice, & Cormier, 2005, p. 19) [or
        "Quinsey, Harris, Rice, and Cormier (2005, p. 19) state
        . . . ."]; thereafter use "(Quinsey et al., 2005, p. 19)"
        [or "Quinsey et al. (2005, p. 19) state . . ."].

R: Quinsey, V. L., Harris, G. T., Rice, M. E., & Cormier,
        C. A. (2005). *Violent offenders: Appraising and
        managing risk* (2nd ed.). New York, NY: American
        Psychological Association.

Note: See the APA style book for information on citing works by
six or more authors.

Books with an Organization as Author

IT: (University of Chicago Press, 2010, p. 655) [or "the Uni-
        versity of Chicago Press (2010, p. 655) states . . ."].

R: University of Chicago Press. (2010). *The Chicago
        manual of style* (16th ed.). Chicago, IL: University
        of Chicago Press.

Chapter in a Multi-Authored Book

Note: In this type of citation, in the reference citation, the chapter
title is provided before the book title, and the inclusive pages of the
chapter are given after the book title.

IT: (Banovetz, 1994, p. 10) [or "Banovetz (1994, p. 10)
        states . . ."].

R: Banovetz, J. M. (1994). The challenges of community
        government. In J. M. Banovetz, D. A. Dolan, & J. W.
        Swain (Eds.), *Managing small cities and counties: A
        practical guide* (pp. 3–27). Washington, DC: Interna-
        tional City/County Management Association.

Journal Articles

Notes: The general format for journal articles is as follows: (1) in the in-text citation, provide last name(s) of author(s) or editor(s), year of publication, and page number of the quotation or point being referenced; (2) in the reference citation, provide last name(s) and first initial(s) of author(s) or editor(s), year of article, title of article, title of journal, volume number of journal, issue number of journal (if available), and inclusive page numbers. Also add DOI or URL if available (see explanation of DOI and URL in previous section).

Journal Article with Single Author

IT: (Rubin, 2007, p. 609) [or "Rubin (2007, p. 609) states . . ."].

R: Rubin, I. (2007). The great unraveling: Federal budgeting, 1998–2006. *Public Administration Review, 67*(4), 608–617.

Journal Article with Two Authors

IT: (Norris & Reddick, 2013, p. 173) [or "Norris and Reddick (2013, p. 173) state . . ."].

R: Norris, D. F., & Reddick, C. G. (2013). Local e-government in the United States: Transformation or incremental change? *Public Administration Review, 72*(1), 165–175. doi:10.1111/j.1540-6210.2012.02647.x [Note: No period after DOI.]

Journal Article with Three to Five Authors

IT: (Cabaleiro, Buch, & Vaamonde, 2013, p. 749) [or "Cabaleiro, Buch, and Vaamonde (2013, p. 749) state . . ."] for first citation in the text; thereafter use "(Cabaleiro et al., 2013, p. 749)" [or "Cabaleiro et al. (2013, p. 749) state . . ."].

R: Cabaleiro, R., Buch, E., & Vaamonde, A. (2013). Developing a method to assessing the municipal financial health. *American Review of Public Administration*, *43*(6), 729–751. doi:10.1177/0275074012451523 [Note: No period after DOI.]

Note: See the APA style book for information on citing works by six or more authors.

Other Common Citations

Magazine Article

IT: (Krakovsky, 2013, p. 29) [or "Krakovsky (2013, p. 29) states . . ."].

R: Krakovsky, M. (2013, November). The words that bind. *Discover*, *34*(9), 28–30.

Newspaper Article

IT: (Ruthhart, 2013, p. 1) [or "Ruthhart (2013, p. 1) states . . ."].

R: Ruthhart, B. (2013, October 12). Speed cameras' potential windfall. *Chicago Tribune*, pp. 1, 4.

Government Document

IT: (U.S. Census Bureau, 2000) [or "the U.S. Census
       Bureau (2000) states . . ."].

R: U.S. Census Bureau. (2000). *Statistical abstract of the
       United States.* Washington, DC: U.S. Government
       Printing Office.

Website

IT: (Clements et al., 2011) [or "Clements et al. (2011)
       state . . ."].

R: Clements, J., Angeli, E., Schiller, K., Gooch, S. C.,
       Pinkert, L., & Brizee, A. (2011, October 12). General
       format. Retrieved October 18, 2013, from http://owl.
       english.purdue.edu/owl/resource/717/13/ [Note:
       No period after URL.]

Blog Entry

IT: (Becker, 2013) [or "Becker (2013) states . . ."].

R: Becker, G. (2013, October 6). Ceilings on government
       debt, taxes, and government spending [Web log
       post]. Retrieved from http://www.becker-posner-
       blog.com/2013/10/ceilings-on-government-debt-
       taxes-and-government-spending-becker.html
       [Note: No period after URL.]

Appendix C

Answers to Exercises

Chapter 1

Exercise 1.1

a. The purpose is to persuade.
b. The audience is the general public.
c. *Answers can vary but should include at least the following:* The message is effective in that it explains how citizens can help with a problem, but it could be improved by providing a reason (or reasons) why the problem exists.

Exercise 1.2

a. The purpose is to inform.
b. The audience is a group of experts.
c. *Answers can vary but should include at least the following:* The paragraph would be better organized if the first two sentences were reversed; as it now appears, the reader does not know what the project is or what "EA" means until the second sentence.

Chapter 2

Exercise 2.1

a. Our training seminar will be ~~complimented~~ *complemented* by small-group breakout sessions.

b. Olivia used official ~~stationary~~ *stationery* to reply to the complaint.

c. Each employee's evaluation session was ~~enlightning~~ *enlightening*.

d. Her manager used poor ~~judgement~~ *judgment* in handling the situation.

e. Each resident filled out a questionnaire. [*Correct as shown*]

f. Tamara's request was granted; she is being ~~transfered~~ *transferred* to the Public Works Department.

g. The mayor renewed her ~~committment~~ *commitment* to a safer environment.

Exercise 2.2

a. The department heads met for an hour; [*delete comma*] and then left.

b. Vehicles with permits can be parked on the street overnight. [*Add period*]

c. The library offered the following classes: Excel, Word, [*insert comma*] and Access.

d. The mayor's top assistant, Dan Pavlicek, [*add commas before and after "Dan Pavlicek"*] sent the e-mail.

e. According to the Department of Health, the new ordinance will help "all residents." [*Move period so it appears before last quotation mark*]

f. The commission referred Mr. Shrader to the proposal, [*insert comma*] which was submitted yesterday. [*Note: If the writer intended this last phrase to be essential to the meaning of the sentence, you would change "which" to "that" and not insert a comma ("The commission referred Mr. Shrader to the proposal that was submitted yesterday.").]*

g. The new center is scheduled to open its doors tomorrow. [*Correct as shown*]

Exercise 2.3

	Original Sentence	Problem/Possible Revision(s)
a.	The new state law prohibits electronics in landfills, they must be recycled.	*Run-on sentence; possible revisions include changing to separate sentences or changing the comma to a semicolon ("The new state law prohibits electronics in landfills. They must be recycled." "The new state law prohibits electronics in landfills; they must be recycled.")*
b.	A workshop on loans are scheduled for Tuesday.	*Subject-verb disagreement; change plural verb "are" to singular verb "is" to match singular subject ("workshop")*
c.	Flu shots will be offered at grocery stores, pharmacies, and in all park district offices.	*Lack of parallelism; change series to all nouns ("Flu shots will be offered at grocery stores, pharmacies, and all park district offices.")*
d.	Because the emergency plans are ready.	*Sentence fragment; either delete subordinating word "Because" or add fragment to independent clause (for example, "Because the emergency plans are ready, we earned an award of recognition.")*
e.	After being ranked a "Top 10 Farmers' Market" in the state, vendor applications for booth space increased.	*Dangling modifier (the vendor applications were not being ranked; the farmers' market was); one possible revision would be "After being ranked a 'Top 10 Farmers' Market' in the state, the Oakdale Farmers' Market experienced an increase in vendor applications for booth space."*
f.	Either the state or the counties within that state are responsible.	*Correct as shown*
g.	Any senior citizen can apply for their discount.	*Subject-pronoun disagreement; change to "Any senior citizen can apply for a discount."*

Chapter 3

Exercise 3.1

Note: Answers can vary; the second column has suggested replacements.

	Original Sentence	Suggested Replacement
a.	The dog owner found a new dog-friendly park for his pet, which was only two blocks away from his house.	*The pet owner found a new dog-friendly park, which was only two blocks away from his house.*
b.	The Accounting Department will endeavor to ascertain the amount of remuneration due to the employee.	*The Accounting Department will determine the amount owed to the employee.*
c.	DHS will hire four hundred more TSA agents by the end of the fiscal year.	*The Department of Homeland Security will hire four hundred more Transportation Security Administration agents by the end of the fiscal year.*
d.	The board argued in favor of downsizing the department.	*The board favored making cuts in the department.*
e.	It is the plan of this office to fund next year's Fourth of July parade.	*This office will fund next year's Fourth of July parade.*
f.	We plan to elucidate the heretofore confusing proposal.	*We will explain the confusing proposal.*

Exercise 3.2

Note: Answers can vary; the second column has suggested replacements.

	Original Sentence	Suggested Replacement
a.	Due to the fact that we are expecting more than five inches of snowfall after 6:00 p.m. tonight, we will implement our snow emergency plan now.	*Because we are expecting more than five inches of snow after 6:00 p.m., we will start our snow emergency plan now.*
b.	The Andrews family is delighted to live in close proximity to the new school.	*The Andrews family is delighted to live close to the new school.*
c.	With this effort, we can take the village to the next level.	*With this effort, we can improve the village.*
d.	Less people came to the hearing than we expected.	*Fewer people came to the hearing than we expected.*
e.	Residents are being urged by city officials to boil their water today.	*City officials urge residents to boil their water today.*
f.	Local policemen arrived at the scene within minutes of the accident.	*Local police officers arrived at the scene within minutes of the accident.*

Exercise 3.3

After the Transportation Committee hearing, many residents remain unhappy with proposed changes to North Street. For example, business owners expressed concern over lost business during the construction period. In addition, residents who live on 16th Street voiced opposition because vehicles would be temporarily rerouted along their street, resulting in increased traffic in a school zone. Nevertheless, the Transportation Committee is set to approve the motion to bring the proposal to the full council.

Chapter 4

Exercise 4.1

FOLLOW US ON TV AND ONLINE

Residents can find out more about village board activities by tuning into cable channel 2 to view board meetings live. meetings are also streamed live on www.grovewood.us/boardtv. The online site also offers a list of archived meetings so you can click on a date and watch a passed meeting.

For more information about these meetings or the village in general, call us at 555-4238. you can also e-mail village@grovewood.us.

Chapter 5

Exercise 5.1

Note: Answers will vary. The memo below is one possible response.

To: All Staff Members
From: Walter Whitman, Technical Support Department
Date: July 25, 2014
Subject: New Copier Codes

Effective August 1, 2014, you will need to start using a new, individually assigned code to operate the copier.

We are making this change for two reasons. First, with this change we will be able to charge each organizational unit for the copying costs it incurs, thus improving our accuracy in accounting for specific costs. Second, by making each unit responsible for its own copying expenses and making each staff member more aware of these expenses, we believe we can reduce overall copying costs.

Your new individual copier code will be sent to you by e-mail on July 31. Please do not share this copier code with any other employee.

Thank you for your cooperation in this matter.

Chapter 6

Exercise 6.1

Note: Answers will vary. The e-mail below is one possible response.

From: Miles Clark
Sent: October 8, 2014
To: Joanna Jarrett and Derek Brown
Subject: Proposal for New Departmental Printer

Dear Joanna and Derek,

I am writing to remind you that I need your feedback on the proposal I sent you last week regarding a new printer for the department. I am meeting with Joe in Purchasing on Friday, so please let me know by the end of today of any changes or additions you wish to make.

I appreciate your prompt response.

Regards,
Miles

Note: The second paragraph in the original e-mail was deleted because of its tone of frustration and because it dealt with a topic completely different from the main subject of the e-mail.

Chapter 7

Exercise 7.1

Correct order of numbered paragraphs: 3, 2, 4, 6, 1, 5

Note: Below we show the news release with the paragraphs in the correct inverted pyramid style, followed by explanations of why each paragraph is placed in the order shown.

NEWS RELEASE
CITY OF MCGUIN
625 North Forest Street
McGuin, NE 68100
Date: June 24, 2014

FOR IMMEDIATE RELEASE

Free Disposal of Hazardous Waste

On Saturday, July 12, McGuin residents can bring their household hazardous waste to McGuin Park for free disposal. The collection will start at 9:00 a.m. and end at 3:00 p.m. McGuin Park is located at 493 East Second Street.

[*This paragraph contains an attention-getting lead sentence and has the information of most interest to the public (who, what, where, and when).*]

Accepted household hazardous waste items are as follows:

- automobile antifreeze
- batteries
- cleaning products
- insecticides
- light bulbs (fluorescent and CFLs)
- paints (oil-based only)

[This paragraph is the next most important because, after knowing the major details, residents will be most interested in what items will be accepted for disposal.]

Items that cannot be accepted include the following:

- business waste
- empty spray cans
- latex paint
- tires

[This paragraph is next because it gives the next most important information, that is, the items that residents should not bring for disposal. (Note: Generally speaking, negative points follow positive points, unless the negative points are clearly more important.)]

Remember that it is illegal to dispose of any hazardous materials in the trash or sewers. Such disposal harms both the environment and anyone who comes into contact with these materials while collecting trash or working on sewers.

[This paragraph is next because it is relevant to the topic of hazardous waste but contains very general information in comparison to the previous two paragraphs.]

Residents can contact Tony Amato in the McGuin Public Works Department for more information on what will and will not be accepted. His telephone number is (611) 555-9823; his e-mail address is tony.amato@mcguin.us.

[This paragraph is last because it just tells residents where they can obtain more information. (Note that the release could be published without this last paragraph [or, if need be, the last two paragraphs] and still provide valuable news to the residents.)]

Media should contact Andrea Wilson in the McGuin Communications Department for more information. Call (611) 555-9834 or e-mail awilson@mcguin.us.

[This paragraph is placed here because media contact information appears after the end of the news portion of the release.]

Chapter 8

Exercise 8.1

Note: Answers will vary. Below are possible responses.

a. Some newsletters might have their text in one column, whereas others might have two or three columns. One might be produced in one or two colors, whereas others might have three or four colors. Some might have pictures or other graphics.
b. All newsletters should have correct spelling and punctuation throughout. The writing should be clear, concise, and coherent, and all articles should be geared toward a general audience.
c. Most newsletters will have a mix of news and feature articles and other information.
d. Numbers will vary, but some newsletters have approximately 75 percent news, 15 percent feature stories, and 10 percent other information (directories of departments, for example).
e. Stories that attract attention will have eye-catching headlines and attention-getting lead sentences. Headlines and lead sentences will most likely have active verbs. The most important articles will start in the top-left and lower-right sections of the first page.
f. The best newsletter will be, first, the one that is most visually appealing, with text set in two or three columns; photos and other illustrations to break up the text; and enough white space between the columns and in the margins to make the pages easily readable. Second, the text itself will most likely be set in serif typeface, and the headings will be set in sans serif typeface. There might be one other color besides black, and that color will be used throughout the newsletter (in the logo and in headings and subheadings, for example) to create cohesiveness. The newsletter will feature a mix of news and feature stories, all well written with eye-catching lead sentences. The sentences themselves will be short and concise, and most will have active verbs to keep the stories interesting. Paragraphs within stories will also be short.

Chapter 9

Exercise 9.1

- Introduction: 3
- Body: 4, 6, 8–13, 16–17
- Conclusion: 5
- Not to be included: 1, 2, 7, 14–15, 18–19

Chapter 10

Exercise 10.1

Note: Answers will vary. The introduction below is one possible response.

> I am writing to suggest that you consider a flexible schedule for employees. I truly believe that the costs would be minimal and that the benefits would be greater productivity and happier employees. Below I will describe what I see as the problems, the solution, the costs, and the benefits.

Exercise 10.2

Note: Answers will vary. Each answer below is one possible response.

a. Title: Employee Suggestion Rewards Program, Employee Rewards for Savings Program, or Employee Suggestion Cost-Savings Rewards Program.
   [Note that all the suggested titles include the words "Employee" and "Rewards" to stress that the main purpose of the program is to motivate employees with rewards.]
b. The problem or opportunity: Because our organization, despite everyone's best efforts, is not perfect, we are spending more than we otherwise might by not using the best

operating methods. In other words, we can spend less to get the same results.

c. The purpose of the proposal: The purpose of this proposal is to encourage employees to think about, find, and suggest ways of making our operations less costly.

d. One or more alternate solutions: The alternate solutions to this proposal include not implementing it and seeking outside expertise.

e. The benefits of the proposed solution: The benefits of this proposed solution include operational cost savings and improved employee morale.

f. The costs of the proposal: The costs include personnel time for program design and promotion, a modest amount for office supplies, and a retainer for an independent accounting firm to calculate cost savings; initial discussions indicate that costs are in the $3,000 to $6,000 range.

Chapter 11

Exercise 11.1

Note: Answers will vary. Each answer below is one possible response.

a. The North-South Serving Seniors Organization requests $250,000 annually for five years to conduct the Assisting Low-Income Seniors with Government Agencies program for the purpose of providing assistance in dealing with government agencies to provide a reduced level of financial and emotional burdens to low-income seniors in North-South County.

b. The North-South Serving Seniors Organization is qualified and a meritorious choice for such funding because it has been providing services to seniors continuously since 1956 as a nonprofit organization recognized by the Internal Revenue Service, the United States Post Office, and the

Secretary of State of the State of Ohio. The North-South
Serving Seniors Organization has successfully administered
forty-eight grant programs totaling more than $100,000,000
in grant funds, including two grants from your foundation
totaling $4,000,000.
c. Need or problem: We have observed that many low-income
seniors pay taxes and fees erroneously, fail to manage the
qualification processes for government-provided benefits,
experience severe anxiety and emotional distress, and
spend many fruitless hours trying to relate to government
agencies that they do not understand.
d. Benefits: The benefits are that seniors served by this program will pay the appropriate taxes and fees to government
agencies, receive the benefits to which they are legitimately
entitled, and live less anxiously and with fewer financial
difficulties.
e. Expenditures: We request funding for three government
assistance agents, one administrative assistant, travel expenses, and telephone service. North-South Serving Seniors
Organization will fund all overhead expenses and other
operating expenses, including administrative supervision,
training, personnel administration, and everything else
necessary for program operations, including office space,
furniture, supplies, and contractual services.

Chapter 12

Exercise 12.1

Note: Answers can vary but should include most of the
following.

a. Details: The personnel salary total of $475,000 includes
one director at $65,000, seven librarians at $50,000 each,
one administrative staff at $35,000, and one custodial staff
at $25,000.

b. Numbers: The employer tax total is calculated by multiplying the personnel salary total ($475,000) by the total of the employer tax rates (12.65 percent), which include FICA (Social Security and Medicare) at 7.65 percent, state and federal unemployment taxes at 3 percent, and workers' compensation at 2 percent.

c. Background: Provides information to the public on-site from 9:00 a.m. to 6:00 p.m. Monday through Saturday and through its website, offers related programing, and is a place where people can gather information and meet. The librarians assist patrons, staff the circulation and reference desks, acquire and manage material, and work with programs. *[Note that the name of the library appears elsewhere in the budget and that the motto is not useful background information, so neither is included here.]*

d. Rationales: Serves the 23,000 residents of Wickgate with information by facilitating the circulation of 126,000 items, 13,000 library visits, and 4,200 answers to reference questions on average annually. Provides a public place for individuals, meetings, and related programming. *[Note that not all of the gathered information was incorporated in the answer because extra information would not add to the effectiveness of your budget justification.]*

Chapter 13

Exercise 13.1

Note: Answers can vary but might include the following.

City of Eastwest
Conduct on City Property Rules

I. Purposes. The purposes of the Conduct on City Property Rules are to allow the public to use public property and to allow the city employees and officials to do their work.

II. Applicability. The City of Eastwest Conduct on City Property Rules apply to all persons on or in city property.
III. Required Conduct
   A. All persons must comply with directives on official signs displayed on city property. Official signs carry the seal of the city.
   B. All persons must comply with directives from city personnel acting in an official capacity. City personnel acting in an official capacity must show their city credentials upon request. City credentials show name, department, and employee number, and they carry the seal of the city.
IV. Prohibited Conduct on City of Eastwest Property
   A. Causing harm to people
   B. Causing harm to city property
   C. Taking city property
   D. Climbing on city property
   E. Disorderly conduct
   F. Gambling
V. Definitions
   A. Climbing on city property refers to when people separate themselves from contact with the walking surface of outside city property, the usual walking surfaces of city facilities, or the customary use of furniture and equipment and suspend themselves above the customarily used surfaces of city property.
   B. Disorderly conduct refers to making loud or unusual sounds, blocking the paths of others, or otherwise interfering with the public's use of city property or the work of city employees.
   C. Gambling refers to engaging in any activity related to wagers or games of chance for money or other things of value. Gambling activities include participating in any fashion in a wager or game of chance, operating gambling devices, or buying or selling lottery tickets.

Notes

Chapter 1

1. See Judith Gillespie Myers, *Plain Language in Government Writing: A Step-by-Step Guide* (Vienna, VA: Management Concepts, 2008), 33.

Chapter 2

1. Lynne Truss, *Eats, Shoots and Leaves: The Zero Tolerance Approach to Punctuation* (New York: Gotham Books, 2004), back cover.

Chapter 3

1. See Joanne Locke, "A History of Plain Language in the United States Government (2004)," accessed October 23, 2013, http://www.plainlanguage.gov/whatisPL/history/locke.cfm. Also see Myers, *Plain Language in Government Writing*, 12, and, for general information on the movement, http://www.plainlanguage.gov.

2. From "Yes Minister Series," website of Jonathan Webb (writer of series), accessed October 20, 2013, http://www.jonathanlynn.com/tv/yes_minister_series/yes_minister_episode_quotes.htm.

Chapter 4

1. Ferris Jabr, "The Reading Brain in the Digital Age: The Science of Paper versus Screens," *Scientific American*, April 11, 2013.

Chapter 6

1. Edwin O. Stene, "Seven Letters: A Case in Public Management," *Public Administration Review* 17, no. 2 (Spring 1957): 83–90.

2. Jabr, "The Reading Brain in the Digital Age."

Chapter 7

1. For the complete list, see "What Are the Most Common Errors Our Editors Catch in Your Press Releases?" BusinessWire, last modified September 4, 2013, http://blog.businesswire.com/2013/09/04/most-common-press-release-errors/.

Chapter 9

1. "Biography of Gene Fowler," accessed March 16, 2014, http://www.imdb.com/name/nm0288706/bio.
2. We thank Judith Gillespie Myers for this point. See Myers, *Plain Language in Government Writing*, 287.

Chapter 11

1. Patrick Henry School of Science and Arts, "Budget Information" (grant proposal), accessed October 26, 2013, http://www2.ed.gov/policy/gen/leg/foia/grants/cspatrickhenryschoolofscienceandarts.pdf.

Annotated Bibliography

Allison, Libby, and Miriam F. Williams. *Writing for the Government*. New York: Pearson Longman, 2008.

> This book focuses on writing in what the authors refer to as the "cultural context" of government documents. That is, the authors discuss how to write various government documents by taking into account such factors as the historical and current political and economic circumstances in which they are produced. Their chapter on grants and proposals is particularly helpful.

Arnold, David S. "Communication." In *Managing Small Cities and Counties: A Practical Guide*, edited by James M. Banovetz, Drew A. Dolan, and John W. Swain, 291–316. Washington, DC: International City/County Management Association, 1994.

> This chapter provides a good overview of the communication skills needed to work effectively with both internal and external audiences who interact with local governments.

Bernstein, Theodore M. *The Careful Writer: A Modern Guide to English Usage*. New York: Atheneum, 1965.

> This book is highly recommended for those who love language and are concerned with proper word usage. It provides an alphabetical listing of certain words and their correct meanings and proper usage. The author is very instructive and humorous at the same time.

BusinessWire. "What Are the Most Common Errors Our Editors Catch in Your Press Release?" Last modified September 4, 2013. http://blog.businesswire.com/2013/09/04/most-common-press-release-errors/.

> This website provides the top ten errors that a wire service sees in press releases. The information is a helpful reminder to writers to check and double-check their media releases before they send them out.

Chen, Greg C., Dall W. Forsythe, Lynne A. Weikart, and Daniel W. Williams. "Presenting the Budget." In *Budget Tools: Financial Methods in the Public Sector*, 101–19. Washington, DC: CQ Press, 2009.

> This chapter focuses especially on writing budget justifications and provides numerous examples. The authors ably explain terms that are likely to be encountered when writing budget justifications.

City of Bellevue (Washington), Finance Department. "Budget." Accessed October 13, 2013. http://www.bellevuewa.gov/budgets.htm.

> This website provides links to a variety of budget documents highly relevant to budget justifications. The page titled "Budget One Request for Results" indicates how the city of Bellevue budgets and also discusses concepts used in budget justifications. Other links lead to documents with many examples of written budget justifications.

Einsohn, Amy. *The Copyeditor's Handbook: A Guide for Book Publishing and Corporate Communications*. Berkeley: University of California Press, 2000.

> This is a good book for beginners in the areas of publishing and communications who want a lot of detail. Einsohn's experience as an editor of scholarly books shows in this volume.

Fowler, H. W. *A Dictionary of Modern English Usage*. 2nd ed. Edited by Ernest Gowers. New York: Oxford University Press, 1965.

> This classic, originally published in 1926, is an invaluable guide to learning proper usage, style, and spelling of words in the English language. As the book jacket says, it is the "famous compilation of learning, wit, humour and good taste."

Garner, Bryan A. *Legal Writing in Plain English*. 2nd ed. Chicago: University of Chicago Press, 2012.

> In this book, Garner, author of the well-known *Modern American Usage*, provides an excellent guide to producing well-written documents, particularly legal documents. Writers who find this book useful might also want to check out his *HBR Guide to Better Business Writing* (2012).

Gordon, Karen Elizabeth. *The Deluxe Transitive Vampire: The Ultimate Handbook of Grammar for the Innocent, the Eager, and the Doomed*. New York: Pantheon Books, 1993.

> A special edition of the classic titled *The Transitive Vampire*, this book about grammar is, as reviewers state, actually fun to read. Gordon uses black humor to illustrate rules; gargoyles, bats, and other creatures fill the pages, too. The first sentence of the book gives an indication of what is to come: "The subject is that part of the sentence about which something is divulged; it is what the sentence's other words are gossiping about."

Human Kinetics. "Proofreading." Accessed October 3, 2013. www.human kinetics.com/flguideonweb/pp42-47.htm.

This website provides valuable tips on how to proofread effectively and efficiently.

Iowa State Legislature. "Rule-Writing Style." Accessed October 3, 2013. https:// www.legis.iowa.gov/DOCS/Rules/Current/StyleGuide.pdf.

This source provides a style guide for writing administrative rules in the state of Iowa, but many of the guidelines will be helpful for anyone who writes rules.

Jabr, Ferris. "The Reading Brain in the Digital Age: The Science of Paper versus Screens." *Scientific American*, April 11, 2013.

This article is a fascinating study of how we read text differently on a computer screen as compared with how we read text on paper. The article is an important reminder to be extra careful when we write and send a communication electronically.

Lehman, Carol M., and Debbie D. Dufrene. *Business Communication*. 16th ed. Mason, OH: South-Western Cengage Learning, 2011.

Although it is geared toward students studying business, this volume gives all readers interesting information on the factors that affect communication in general, and it provides good general guidelines on writing various types of documents.

May, Debra Hart. *Proofreading Plain and Simple*. Franklin Lakes, NJ: Career Press, 1997.

As the title implies, this book provides some basic tips on and techniques for proofreading. It also contains helpful advice on basic editing.

Merriam-Webster's Collegiate Dictionary. 11th ed. Springfield, MA: Merriam-Webster, 2003.

This dictionary is a standard in the publishing industry. The CD-ROM included with the book offers instant accessibility to all the words in the printed form.

MLA Handbook for Writers of Research Papers. 7th ed. New York: Modern Language Association, 2009.

This style book is used by many students and scholars in the humanities. In addition to providing guidelines on the Modern Language Association's documentation style, the book has excellent information on how to write research papers.

Myers, Judith Gillespie. *Plain Language in Government Writing: A Step-by-Step Guide.* Vienna, VA: Management Concepts, 2008.

> This book focuses on how to write more plainly (as the author notes, she was inspired by the plain language movement). Although it is geared toward writers in the federal government, the book is a good resource for writers in all levels of government.

Plain Language Action and Information Network. "Federal Plain Language Guidelines." Last modified May 2011. http://www.plainlanguage.gov/index.cfm.

> This website is a valuable resource for all writers who want to express themselves more clearly. The team who created the network originally focused on writing regulations, but they have broadened the guidelines to include other forms of communication.

Publication Manual of the American Psychological Association. 6th ed. Washington, DC: American Psychological Association, 2009.

> This style book is used by many students and scholars in the social and behavioral sciences as the primary guide for citing references. In addition, it provides guidelines on other aspects of the writing process, including how to write effective manuscripts.

Redish, Janice. *How to Write Regulations and Other Legal Documents in Clear English.* Washington, DC: American Institutes for Research Document Design Center, 1991.

> This book provides practical advice for writing rules in a clear fashion. It emphasizes thinking about audiences, understanding how audiences will use the rules, and thinking about how rules can be written for specific audiences.

Sabin, William A. *The Gregg Reference Manual: A Manual of Style, Grammar, Usage, and Formatting.* 11th ed. New York: McGraw-Hill, 2011.

> Regarded as one of the better manuals for business professionals, this book is written in easy-to-understand language and covers the basics.

Stene, Edwin O. "Seven Letters: A Case in Public Management." *Public Administration Review* 17, no. 2 (Spring 1957): 83–90.

> As mentioned in the text, this classic article exemplifies what can go wrong when communications among an organization's colleagues are not clear. It is especially valuable for showing what happens when we do not understand our roles and interests and the roles and interests of others in our organization.

Strunk, William, Jr., and E. B. White. *The Elements of Style*. 4th ed. Boston: Allyn and Bacon, 2000.

> Termed "timeless" and a classic, this slim volume covers useful rules of grammar and style, with an emphasis on clarity and conciseness in writing.

Truss, Lynne. *Eats, Shoots and Leaves: The Zero Tolerance Approach to Punctuation*. New York: Gotham Books, 2004.

> As noted earlier in the text, this book was a surprise best seller when it was published. It is written with humor and makes a strong case for the importance of punctuation.

University of Chicago Press. *The Chicago Manual of Style*. 16th ed. Chicago: University of Chicago Press, 2010.

> Considered by many writers and editors to be the bible of the publishing industry, this book is, as its jacket states, an "indispensable reference for writers, editors, proofreaders, indexers, copywriters, designers, and publishers." The book covers every aspect of publishing and is geared toward those in that field.

U.S. Geological Society. "Proofreading." Accessed October 18, 2013. http://www.nwrc.usgs.gov/techrpt/sta33.pdf.

> This link offers a good general overview of proofreading and provides suggestions on how to proofread more effectively.

U.S. National Archives and Records Administration, Office of the Federal Register. "Plain Writing Tools." Accessed October 12, 2013. http://www.archives.gov/federal-register/write/plain-language/index.html.

> This website provides links to several useful resources, including "Making Regulations Readable," "Drafting Legal Documents," and "Rewriting a Short Rule: Step by Step." The website also links to the *Code of Federal Regulations* and the *Federal Register*.

Wheeler, Kenneth M., ed. *Effective Communication: A Local Government Guide*. Washington, DC: International City/County Management Association, 1994.

> One of the many excellent volumes in International City/County Management Association's Municipal Management Series, this book describes various areas of local government where good communication skills are required and provides helpful guidelines on ways to implement effective communication in those areas. Of special interest might be the chapters titled "Working with the News Media" and "Local Government Publications."

Wienbroer, Diana Roberts, Elaine Hughes, and Jay Silverman. *Rules of Thumb for Business Writers*. 2nd ed. New York: McGraw-Hill, 2005.

> This book is an excellent resource for solving specific writing problems, and it is written in an easy-to-understand style.

Williams, Robin. *The Non-Designer's Design Book: Design and Typographic Principles for the Visual Novice*. 3rd ed. Berkeley, CA: Peachpit Press, 2008.

> In a lighthearted way, this basic book about design and typography principles is very helpful, especially for those who do not have any background in design but need a little guidance to put a newsletter or brochure together in a visually appealing way.

Index

Note: Italic page numbers with *f* indicate figures and with *t* indicate tables.

About the Authors

John W. Swain has taught public administration courses for more than thirty-five years. He has also provided training to and worked with a wide variety of staff members, administrators, and officials in the public sector. His previously published books focus on public budgeting, public finance administration, and local government. He holds a bachelor's degree in political science from the University of New Hampshire and master's and doctoral degrees in political science from Northern Illinois University.

Kathleen Dolan Swain has been an editor for more than twenty years, working primarily in the field of scholarly publishing. She has also worked extensively in the development of curriculum materials and has written news and feature articles for local news outlets. She holds a bachelor's degree in political science and history from Marquette University and a master's degree in political science from Northern Illinois University.

The authors offer workshops on the tips and techniques for better writing discussed in this book. They can be contacted at www. wordmatterschicago.com.